Violet

The Canadian Lieutenant's Wife

Violet

The Canadian Lieutenant's Wife

by Roger Sherburn-Hall

Violet – the Canadian Lieutenant's Wife

First published 2022

Published by Roger Sherburn-Hall
rogersherburnhall@btinternet.com

Typeset by John Owen Smith

© Roger Sherburn-Hall

Credits

a. Much advice, encouragement given by local historian and creative wordsmith, John Owen Smith. (www.johnowensmith.co.uk).
b. The staff at the Liphook Heritage Centre were a great source of information, always friendly and helpful. (www.liphookheritage.org.uk)
c. My wife Ann, who has inspired and encouraged me throughout.

Dedicated to

- Violet Hall and her husband Frank and to all those of my family who have gone before me.
- Alan Scott Hall, (my eldest son) who was born on 29th October 1974 and tragically died on 23rd June 2008.

Contents

Introduction to Violet

That's me up there with my mum and two sisters, enjoying our life in 1951! I never would have believed that I might write a book or enjoy the research and accomplishment so much.

I thought that a lot had happened to me during my life, but like everyone else we wouldn't be here unless our ancestors paved the way. In doing so they had adventures and experiences that we in this ever safer, tamer world can only gasp at.

I have found during my 32 years as a policeman, that some experiences harden our sensitivities. I once specialized in dealing with people who had died. (Three or four a week, in all sorts of circumstances). A friend of mine spent years investigating child abuse. (Far longer than he should have done). Today I retain a macabre sense of (coping) humour that only people with similar backgrounds understand. (I was a soldier for eight years too and I am sure that doesn't help in my relating to 'ordinary people').

People today refer to shell shock, as Post Traumatic Stress Disorder or P.T.S.D. My grandad Frank knew all about it. He was gassed after spending two years in the Western Front in a Canadian infantry battalion that suffered a 91.5% casualty rate. Would you come out of that the same as you went in?

I loved my Nanna as I think did every other child she had dealing with.

(For goodness' sake she introduced me to drinking Guinness and taught me how to use a sewing machine!) When I was with her, I never thought about the life she had lived, until I found the skein of wool in her loft.

My research, (aided by my lovely, clever wife Ann) has unravelled the whole ball.

Roger Sherburn Hall
January 2022

****

Chapter 1

Violet Furlonger's Family

Clutching the big bag of Khaki wool, I clattered eagerly downstairs. I was bursting to ask Nanna about my mysterious find. She was in the lounge, as usual, busily treadling her sewing machine. (Her first Singer had been a gift from her mother in 1910, when she was training to be a dressmaker).

"Nanna, what is this?.....OH OUCH!"
"Roger you silly boy, how many times have I told you to wear your shoes in my workroom? There are pins all over the floor. Come here and let me see your poor little toe".

Sitting on her knee seventy years ago, I can sharply recall Nanna telling me about her brothers and cousins, who had so eagerly joined up during the Great War. Of how they and their mates had suffered from the cold in the waterlogged, sand-bagged, freezing trenches. They served and shivered in places with strange names, like Mons, Cambrai, and Passchendaele. She remembered the long nights in the very same lounge where we sat, knitting, and knitting and knitting.

She produced hundreds of mittens, gloves, scarves, and cardigans over the four years of that terrible conflict.

Nanna described to me making up parcels of these woollens each night, using strong brown paper, labelled, then bound with stout sisal string. Inside each package she enclosed her handwritten note of encouragement. The next morning, she carried the consignments to the Post Office, for shipment to the Army in France.

Some of the soggy mittens are no doubt, to this day buried on those same blasted battlefields, with the remains of the boys who wore them. One of Nanna's favourites was her cousin Arthur, who lived just up the road. He was killed in 1917, whilst serving in the Tank Corps at the Battle of Cambrai. Arthur left his wife Mary as a widow. He was followed in 1918 by George who died at Etaples, while serving as a Private in the Machine Gun Corps. He had been a neighbouring cousin who had been a play-friend of Violet's when they were at school together.

The skein that I had found whilst rummaging in my Nanna's dark loft was a poignant relic. A mournful memory from an anxious and sometimes sad part of her life.

Emma Waring (Violet's mother)

My Grandmother was Violet Kate Furlonger. She lived at 34 Kings Road, Haslemere, in the county of Surrey. Her home was a three-bedroomed detached family house, and it was situated alongside the busy London to Portsmouth Railway line. I well recall as a child being lulled to sleep in the back bedroom, to the sounds of steam trains snorting and stressing as they puffed to and from Haslemere Station.

'Weybrook', King's Road, Haslemere (Violet's parent's home)

This girl from Haslemere came into the world in 1893. It was during Queen Victoria's reign when William Gladstone was the Prime Minister, and in the same year that Robert Louis Stevenson died. Violet was the first born of Charles and Emma Furlonger (née Waring), who had married a year previously.

Emma came from far away village of Dorstone on the Welsh borders of Herefordshire. The daughter of a sheep farmer and one of four children, she worked as a domestic servant from the age of fourteen. When Emma was twenty-one, she had earned local admiration for putting out a housefire with her bare hands. (Unfortunately, her employer failed to thank her in any way for her bravery. Ever since then, the resentment felt because of this omission has been passed down the generations).

Violet's father, Charles Furlonger, was a 23-year-old coach driver, living in Haslemere when he proposed to Emma, whose home was 150 miles away. (Whether or not their meeting was in connection with his job as a carrier, is something that can now only be open to speculation).

In his role as a husband, Charles spent £500 buying land in Kings Road Haslemere and building a house there. The property had a stream running through the garden, and Charles named the house "Weybrook."

My Grandmother's only sibling was a brother with the name of Walter, (but throughout his life he was always referred to as 'Boy'). He was born three years after she was. They were both baptised at the nearby St Bartholomew's Church.

Violet was very fortunate to have been born into the Furlonger family. They were first recorded hundreds of years ago as residents of the archetypical little English village of Chiddingford, which is about five miles from Haslemere. The Parish was famous for its high-quality coloured glass industry, the origins of which stretch back to the days of the Romans. During the 1800s the village was well-regarded for its cottage industry, making walking sticks and umbrellas for urban markets.

Chiddingfold is situated in rich well-watered faming land and Violet's forebears owned several small farms in the locality.

One of Violet's great uncles in Chiddingfold

In days gone by, despite the high infant mortality rate, it was normal for families to include a lot more children than is the case today. In order to keep the farms intact, it was common for the eldest son to inherit the complete farm upon his father's death. This often incurred a degree of financial hardship on the beneficiary's brothers and sisters. To counter this, the Furlongers developed additional family businesses that complemented the farm and served the local farming community. With this diversification, the younger son's financial futures were nourished and enhanced. Consequently, the extended Furlonger family had enterprises including the Chiddingfold Butchers shop and a Carters firm (transporter of goods). They also owned the village inn, The Crown. (This has existed since the early 1400s and is today a lovely place to visit).

__The Crown in Chiddingfold__

A small parish can only accommodate commercial expansion to a limited extent, and so the family's interests developed into the wider surrounds and away from its original base. Chronicles show that over the years the Furlonger progeny migrated to places such as Hambledon and to Frensham and Haslemere; all of them are in Surrey. One of the sons who moved to Haslemere in the late 19th century opened there a second butcher's shop in the High Street.

After Violet's birth, her father Charles co-founded a general carrier's firm in partnership with a much older entrepreneur who he knew well. The business was called 'Funnell & Furlonger', and their yard and offices were in nearby Grayshott village. Charles, in his early 20s, would have needed a great deal of money by the values of the day to afford this. In addition to getting married at a young age and later building his new house, one can only speculate as to how much the extended Furlonger family assisted with the costs.

As a little girl Violet and her father were very attached to each other. He liked to have her spend time with him, at the office of his by now well-established business. From an early age she ran messages for her father, often calling at the counter of the nearby Grayshott Post Office. Her grandmother (Emma's mother) died in 1898, when Violet was five.

Violet Furlonger aged 15

At 15, Violet left school to begin training as a dressmaker at Tartar's Dress Shop in Guildford. This involved travelling on her own six days a week by train, to and from her workplace.

The first World War started in July 1914 when Violet was 21 years old and still living with her parents. She had developed into a confident and forthright young woman who was, by now, skilled in her trade. She had her own business, making clothes at home for well-to-do customers. Whenever she had the time, she got a lift or cycled the four-mile journey into Grayshott to help at her father's yard. It must have been an exciting time for Violet and her friends with the influx of newly enlisted soldiers into the locality.

By 1915 her brother 'Boy' was eighteen and working for Charles as a van driver. Spurred on by the country's overwhelming patriotism, he enlisted into the army. He did this at the Winchester city recruitment office to become a cyclist in the Hampshire Yeomanry. In those days when motor transport and radio communication were in their infancy, the military often made use of messengers to pass important and confidential despatches. These heralds had a vital and responsible job. Fortunately for him, Walter did not see active service as he was in a second line unit. However, he was sent with his unit to Southern Ireland in the lead up to the Irish War of Independence. There he performed a similar important function on a motorcycle.

Charles Furlonger (Violet's father)

*One of Walter's workmates at the Grayshott yard signed up for the Royal Artillery in 1914 at the age of 14. He stretched the truth about his birthday a lot, because the minimum age for enlistment at that time was 18. However, his work with Funnell and Furlongers had taught him a lot about horses. Men with such skills were in urgent demand by the Army, to work the horses that pulled the guns. Consequently, he was told by the recruiting sergeant to, **"go outside and think carefully about your age son"**.*

He subsequently served 4 years in France before returning to England, amazingly unscathed, aged just 18. This man then resumed working for Violet's father. (I met him as an old man, when I was the village Policemen in Grayshott during the early 1980s. We had a long and interesting talk and he recounted to me some of his experiences, both in and since his army service).

(See also note 1)

After Walter's discharge in 1919, he too resumed his job with his father and lived the rest of his life at the family home at Weybrook.

****

Chapter 2

Frank Hall's family

My paternal Grandfather was Frank Sherburn Hall. His parents, William, and Annie Elizabeth, lived in the small town and river port of Goole, near Hull. This is located in the eastern side of England's largest county of Yorkshire. Frank was born there in 1888 and was one of five sons and seven daughters.

Frank's mother, Annie, came from nearby Sherburn village and her father's name was curiously, George Sherburn. Annie's mother was called Elizabeth Firth and she never married George. Never-the-less she and George lived with each other and had five children together. When Annie was born her mother Elizabeth gave her own name to her baby as a middle name. George gave Annie his surname of Sherburn.

Annie Elizabeth grew up to be a very strong-minded woman. Perhaps it was an early belief in emancipation that caused her to include her maiden name (Sherburn) in each one of her son's names.

East Yorkshire society in the latter half of the 19th century was experiencing great changes fuelled by increasing industrialisation. Coal mined locally powered steam engines which replaced hand and horse-power. Increasingly, tasks, were done by machine. Consequently, many families who had laboured on the land for generations, moved into urban areas in pursuit of work. This surplus of labour resulted in lower wages, unemployment, poor living conditions and growing poverty for working class people. One result was a steady stream of emigrants who were drawn to the open prairies of opportunity on the other side of the Atlantic.

However, there was some work to be had in Yorkshire, servicing the growing middle classes. In the U.S.A., Isaac Merritt Singer invented and then began marketing his sewing machines in 1851. Singer machines were a huge improvement on their predecessors and enabled the production of fashionable clothing at a fraction of previous costs. William Hall (Frank's father), was one of those who as a young man, recognised this opportunity and started his own small drapery business, in Goole.

Clothing fashion in this period was a way for the better off to ostentatiously display their wealth and social status. It was a growth industry.

Expanding affluence allowed an increase in the participation of sporting activities. Popular were rowing, athletics, football, boxing, wrestling, fencing, horse riding, swimming, and bicycling. The Victorians were keen to encourage "manly exercise" and saw it as essential to the building up of a strong character.

Many now famous Yorkshire football clubs came into being during this time. (Sheffield Wednesday 1867, Rotherham United 1870, Barnsley Football Club 1887, and Sheffield United in 1889). The Football Association was formed in 1863, to "establish a definite code of rules for the regulation of the game".

Also, in 1863 the extraordinarily successful Yorkshire Cricket Club was formed, and in 1880 the first cricket test match to take place in Britain was held. In this match the Grace Brothers helped England to win against Australia.

During this changing environment Frank's brother Harry, who had an interest in drawing, studied for two years at the Manchester School of Art. Whilst there he became a member of the English International Water Polo team. In addition to that he made a name for himself as an amateur footballer and boxer.

Frank therefore grew up in a setting where it was expected that young men would be active in one or more sport. He therefore involved himself in athletics, and whilst practicing this suffered an injury to his back which caused him trouble in later life.

After leaving school my grandfather started work for his father as a shop assistant. Shortly before his 16th birthday in 1904, his elder sister Ethel (then aged 21), married a local man called Sidney Smart, and they crossed the Atlantic to settle in far-away Seattle. Later that same year, Frank showed similar independent spirit by signing up for ten years in the Royal Navy. He left home to complete his initial training at HMS Pembroke.

At that time and since 1890 an arms race had been taking place between Germany and Britain, which was to last up to the First World War. This was due to the German ambition to outdo the British Naval strength, and thus force British territorial concessions (i.e. they were envious of our Empire). To add to the picture, Russia was at war with Japan. Furthermore, the recent introduction of submarines (1901) and torpedoes were causing great tactical and design challenges.

Major reforms were taking place within the Royal Navy and to British foreign policy. Government funding for ships doubled, and although Britain had by far the biggest fleet in the world, it was to grow with each passing year.

With this backdrop, the British Government started a huge recruitment drive for Naval recruits. It is not surprising that young Frank was attracted from the job at his father's shop.

On the night of 21/22 October 1904, Frank was on a two-year course at HMS Caledonia, training to qualify as a signalman. That night a notorious accident (forever after referred to as 'The Dogger Bank Incident') occurred near to Frank's hometown. The Baltic Fleet of the Imperial Russian Navy was passing through the North Sea, en-route to the Pacific Ocean. Mistaking a fleet of British trawlers based in Hull, for Japanese Naval torpedo boats, the Russians fired on them. This resulted in one fishing boat being sunk and two fishermen being killed.

Hearing about this must surely have increased young Frank's enthusiasm for his new role.

In 1906, now a qualified signalman, Frank was posted to the modern Drake-class armoured cruiser HMS Good Hope.

After training Frank was posted onto HMS Good Hope

"To keep the sailors' morale high at sea", it was the practice at that time for the ship's administrative Officer (the Purser) to order the piping of "Up Spirits" at noon each day. This told the crew to gather and be issued with a tot of rum (one eighth of a pint at 54.6% strength). The grog was to be drunk, under supervision, at once and 'Jack Tars' in those days got very accustomed to their daily tot of strong drink.

More instructional courses followed, and Frank was next posted onto destroyer depot ships. Firstly, HMS Leander and then on to HMS Blake. He continued his service on HMS Orion, a depot ship for torpedo boats, based at Malta. It is there that he contracted malaria in 1909. One possible long-term effect of having malaria is suffering from depression later in life. As a seaman Frank followed the matelots practice and acquired tattoos on his arm. One of them on was "FH & EW". (I would love to know who EW was and how he met her!)

Throughout his service in the Navy, Frank's conduct was consistently reported as "Very Good", and as a result he was awarded the Good Conduct Badge on 14/4/09. Despite doing well in the senior service, Frank deserted the Navy in 1912, when he was 24 years old. He went to live in Canada.

* * * * * * * * * * * * * * * * * * * *

Chapter 3

The Hall Family's Emigration

On Wednesday the 10th of April 1912, a Trans-Atlantic passenger ship owned by the White Star Line left Southampton Docks on her maiden voyage, bound for New York. At that time, she was the largest passenger ship in the world. The experts proudly reported that her state-of-the-art design made the ship 'unsinkable'. This magnificent vessel was the RMS Titanic. Many of this huge liner's passengers were emigrants on their way to a new life in the U.S.A. or in Canada. Late on the fourth night of the crossing ,in freezing cold weather, the ship was steaming at near full speed 370 miles off the coast of Newfoundland. Quite unexpectedly she struck a huge iceberg, and the 46,328-ton ship began her awful journey to the seabed 12,600 feet below. Only then did the passengers learn that the lifeboats could accommodate only half of those on board. Two hours forty minutes after the collision, and before any other ships could arrive to attempt a rescue, the Titanic sunk. 1,500 people drowned in a sea temperature of -2°.

Seven months after this widely publicised disaster, Frank's parents (then aged 53 and 58 respectively), accompanied by six of their unmarried sons and daughters, left their Yorkshire hometown for good. Having each paid their $20 fare, they boarded the White Star Line RMS Megantic at Liverpool Docks.

Along with hundreds of other nervous but eager emigrants, this brave family left England to begin a new life in Canada. Frank's mother, Annie Elizabeth, had born 14 children during her marriage to William. (She is thought to have had two babies who did not survive infanthood). William had sold up his drapery business to start afresh in the new world. With them went their sons, Harry (22), Fred (23), and Gerald (18), and their daughters Edith (25), Gladys (20), Dorothy (16) and Evelyn (13).

When the trans-Canadian railway line was being built during the late 1800s, the Canadian Pacific Railway (C.P.R.) company had found it unprofitable to put a line right across the prairies, as few people lived there.

Eventually it became necessary for the Government to transport military units across large distances to fight rebellions with indigenous peoples. Only then did they realize how vital was railway for the efficient governance and commerce of their huge country.

As a result of this, the Government saw that it was necessary to increase the country's population especially in the sparsely settled prairies.

They had, for years prior to the Hall's arrival, been encouraging emigration. Part of their tactics in this was to incentivize the C.P.R. by selling them huge quantities of fertile but unfarmed land, at bargain prices.

The C.P.R. saw that they could make huge profits when this rich land were settled and farmed. They thus formed a plan to ease the passage for suitable people to settle in Canada.

This they did by advertising for immigrants right across Europe, and by buying shares in shipping companies. They then subsidized the passenger fares to Canada. In addition, they provided trains with suitably adapted carriages, to transport the incomers right across the country to their destinations. Once they had arrived, the settlers were offered cheap land to buy and for some of them, to farm.

Early on the morning of the 17th of November 1912, after an eight-day voyage across the North Atlantic, the R.M.S. Megantic steamed slowly into Quebec harbour.

R.M.S. Megantic

The Hall family, with hundreds of others, disembarked down the gangplank onto the bustling quayside. After collecting their mountain of luggage, they were soon at the adjacent C.P.R. rail station.

There they were efficiently directed to a special 'Colonist' Passenger Car. It was one of many which were to be pulled behind a huge steam powered, log fuelled, locomotive.

After having bought their travelling food supplies at the railroad store, they were allotted their own family area, which had a kitchen, a stove and bunk beds. Later that same day, in response to flag waving and a loud bell ringing, the train jerked and chuffed to a start.

As it left the railroad station, it puffed and strained westwards, on the long journey across the vast landscape. The Halls looked through their windows, soaking up the strange evolving panorama of their new country. As they did so they soon met and made friends with their travelling companions.

At midday, after a long tiring five-day journey, there was a long, loud, metallic squeal of brakes, before the train shuddered to a stop in Saskatchewan. In the hissing silence they saw that they had arrived at the wooden platform of a small prairie town. Gazing out of the windows they could see for a long way in all directions. The countryside was flat and seemingly featureless, except for the large river alongside which the town had been sited.

Central Moose Jaw in the year that the Halls arrived

The conductor strode quickly through the carriages announcing, "Moose Jaw" in a loud Canadian accent. The Halls were over 4000 miles from their starting place in Goole.

Waving frantically on the platform and running towards them was their 24-year-old son Frank, who had preceded them.

* * * * * * * * * * * * * * * * * * * *

Chapter 4

Settling into Saskatchewan

In 1882, when the C.P.R. was constructing the rail-line right across Canada, they needed plentiful water and wood to fuel their locomotives. It was here beside the Moose Jaw River that they found all that they needed to create a regional base.

When the Hall family finished their long train journey 30 years later, the operations base had developed to become a small frontier town. It is located in the Province of Saskatchewan, 96 miles north of the U.S.A. border and 500 miles east of the Rocky Mountains.

In 1912, fuelled by a flood of settlers, the town was developing at a fast rate. Many people came directly from England, but a lot of Americans from a dozen states came as well. In addition, there were immigrants from Ireland, Scotland, Germany, Norway, Sweden, China and people with French origins from Eastern Canada. English however was the common language.

__The economy was based on growing crops__

In 1912 the C.P.R. had plenty of inexpensive land for sale and many of the newcomers became farmers. They grew chiefly wheat, flax, and oats in the very fertile soil. Farming virgin soil was extremely hard work. Nevertheless, to bring under cultivation their own land was an opportunity they would never have had in their old countries.

There was other work too. The town was booming and had three schools, eight banks, seven hotels, a flour mill, brewery, brick yard, livery and stables, nursery, and grocery, shoe, drug, and hardware shops. There was in addition, an iron machine works, two daily newspapers, a telephone system, and nine churches.

Life in a prairie town

Frank had prepared a home for them all to live in at 112 Larch Avenue, not far from the town centre. The Hall family quickly settled in and found employment in the town.

William snr (aged 58) found familiar work as the manager at Herbert Snell's Ladies wear department store. Fred (aged 31) became a salesman, Florence (29) got work as a nurse, whilst Gladys (20) and Dorothy (17) worked as telephone clerks. Evelyn (13) started her new school, while her brothers Frank (24), Harry (22) and Gerald (18) found jobs on the Canadian Pacific Railway as mail transfer clerks.

Before long the eldest Hall brother, Fred, left Canada to follow his own dream some 800 miles to the south, in Nebraska U.S.A.

As time went along, the remaining older 'children' of the family found independent accommodation in Moose Jaw town. Evelyn and Gladys stayed with their parents at the family home in Larch Avenue.

Gladys before long was dating a young man called Wellington McNab. Florence became fond of a man called WRAY who lived nearby. She was eventually to marry him, and they moved to settle in a small 'village' called Conquest, some 100 miles northwest of Moose Jaw.

****

25

Chapter 5

The build-up to War

The 1876 Battle of Little Big Horn was a fierce encounter between assembled Sioux warriors and Colonel George Custer's U.S. Cavalry unit, in Montana. One of the significant consequences of that momentous event was that 5,000 Native American Indians escaped north across the border, into Canada's Southern Saskatchewan. The Sioux leader was an imposing chief called Sitting Bull. He and his people settled in the Cypress Hills region close to the Northwest Mounted Police base at Fort Walsh. This was just 30 miles south of the trans-Canada railroad.

A group of Saskatchewan First Nation people 1912

At that time, the Canadian Government in Ottawa was encouraging immigration into the underpopulated prairie regions. They wanted it farmed and that clashed with the wishes of the buffalo hunting Native Peoples. (The resultant tension mirrored what was happening in the United States). The Sioux were not welcomed and after a time most had no option but to return across the border.

(One of them, however, who stayed in Canada was a Lakota Sioux squaw named Tasinaskawin Brule. She was the wife of a significant warrior called Black Bull who had died of his wounds. Black Bull's wife had become close friends with a woman of influence from Moose Jaw, called Annie Wallis. When years later Tasinaskawin herself died, she left all she owned to her friend Annie. Her belongings consisted of 7 ponies, a tepee,

a wagon, several blankets, and large quantity of beads.)

One outcome of the Sioux incursion and of other events, was a decision by the Canadian Government, to increase its military resources and re-appraise their disposition.

Linking up the whole country, the newly built railroad afforded fast transport across the prairies. Moose Jaw, being a major rail junction, was one of the towns chosen as a convenient 'Strategic Location', at which to base a Militia unit.

By the early 1900s, part-time army (Militia) regiments, had been formed throughout Canada, each based in a barracks (known as armouries in Canada).

The present Moose Jaw armoury was first built in 1907 and was much improved in 1913/14. When completed it was a substantial and imposing building which had offices, classrooms, a drill hall, mess halls, recreational facilities, and arms and equipment vaults. From 1913 the resident town's Militia unit was the 60th Rifles of Canada, an infantry formation. It was commanded by Lieutenant Colonel (Lt.Col.) Herbert SNELL.

This 35-year-old commanding officer was a man of slight stature, but winning and strong personality. He was born in Stocksbridge, Yorkshire in 1880, and had arrived in Ontario, Canada, aged 11, with his parents. Herbert completed his education at a private school, before starting work in his father's business. At the age of 24 he married Jessie and moved to Moose Jaw in 1909. There Herbert started his own ladies wear retail business. In this he was successful and became a well-regarded town Alderman.

During 1914 the country's Government in Ottawa had been following the worrying events 5,000 miles away but didn't anticipate the possible consequences for Canada.

The country's small part-time army Militia units was not at all professional and reflected the Government's lack of a perceived threat to the nation. At that time, the country had a tiny navy, no Air Force, and maintained just 3,100 full time soldiers. This was despite Canada being the third largest country in the world, and 40 times the size of Britain.

Showground events were a very popular form of entertainment

27

The South Saskatchewan weather in late summer of 1914 was glorious. Every town's focus was on their local country fair. Each year it started off with a parade through the main street, leading the excited townsfolk to their showground.

There they took part in or watched the rodeo and were able to see scores of other amusements.

For months during that year the newspapers had been reporting lurid stories about the life and times of a notorious Canadian criminal. The Hall family and indeed most Canadians had been transfixed by the unfolding tale.

The object of their interest was one Jack Krafchenko, an immigrant from Romania, who had been born in 1881. Krafchenko's misdeeds over many years cast Bonny and Clyde, twenty years later, as relatively minor offenders.

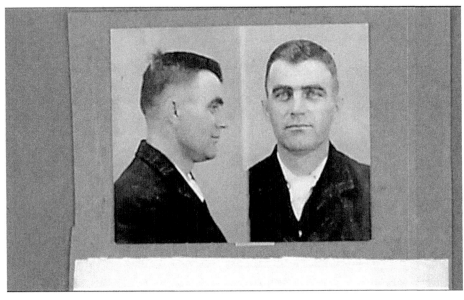

Jack Krafchenko's police "Mug shots"

Krafchenko's own mother had been a horse thief in Greece. He in turn progressed to committing multiple armed bank robberies in Canada, the U.S.A., even in England, Germany, and Italy. He also found the time to be an internationally famous professional boxer and wrestler.

Somehow or other Krafchenko also found time to become a bigamist and to make several spectacular escapes from justice, including one from prison. Eventually he was arrested for murdering a bank manager and, after a well-publicised trial, Krafchenko was hanged on the 9th of July 1914.

Manitoba Free Press

KRAFCHENKO CONDEMNED TO HANG AT WINNIPEG JULY 9

Counsel Will Not Enter Appeal

With all this going on, Canadians watched the unfolding events in Europe with a detached interest.

They were astounded when Great Britain declared war on 28th July 1914. Canada, as a member of the British Empire, followed suit six days later.

EXTRA! No. 2—4:30 p. m. EXTRA!

THE VANCOUVER DAILY PROVINCE

Britain and Germany Now at War

Reuter's Cable Company Makes This Announcement Tonight

The Canadian Government began to assemble an Army

****

Chapter 6

Canada at War

Immediately after the 1914 declaration of war, Canada's controversial Minister for Militia, Sam Hughes, put out a countrywide call for military recruits.

<u>Sir Samuel Hughes, KCB PC, Minister of Militia and Defence</u>
<u>In office 10 October 1911 – 12 October 1916</u>

Hughes himself held the rank of Colonel and had seen active service with the Canadian Militia during the Second Boer War.

There was a huge wave of patriotism right across the country, and young men, excited at the chance of earning valour on the battlefield, clamoured to enlist. (At that time, academic experts unanimously predicted that a modern war could not last more than a few months). Men wanted to 'do their bit' before it was all over.

Posters like this were displayed throughout Saskatchewan

Thus, in late 1914, Colonel Snell (the commander of the Moose Jaw Militia), received instructions from the Ministry of Defence, to increase the recruitment of soldiers. A steady flow of volunteers swelled the ranks of the 60th Rifles at the town Armoury.

__Moose Jaw Armoury__

__Colonel Herbert Snell 1915__

Contrary to popular supposition, young Canadians of those days were not all fit, wholesome, frontiersmen. There was widespread ill health within the population. High numbers took no exercise, lived in unhealthy city slums, and/or had a poor diet. Sexually Transmitted Disease (S.T.D.) was rife, as was tuberculosis and poor eyesight. 4.5% of the general population suffered from syphilis. (An incurable disease, as this was 14 years before the discovery of penicillin).

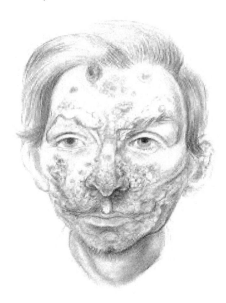

__Some visual effects of suffering in an advanced stage of syphilis__

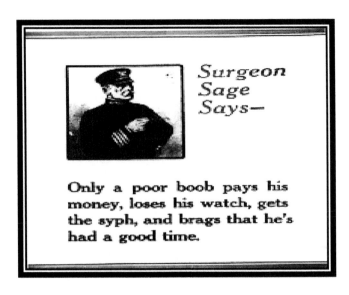

Surgeon Sage Says—

Only a poor boob pays his money, loses his watch, gets the syph, and brags that he's had a good time.

The standard of admittance to the Forces was high, and thousands of volunteers were rejected.

Fit fellows with previous military service were favoured. Initially about 70% of those who joined the country's new army, were British born. Entrants did also include immigrants from other European countries, the U.S.A., and some First Nation peoples. As the casualties of war mounted, the need for replacements increased dramatically. Standards were dropped to meet the demand and between 1914 and 1918 the Canadian Expeditionary Force (C.E.F.) recruited a total of 630,000 men. It was shown that, during the whole of the war, just 50% of those who signed up were Canadian born.

Although initially it had been thought that there was a negligible chance of Canada becoming involved in any wars, these part-time soldiers were sent off to training camp for a week of manoeuvrers each summer. Young men were drawn to join the unit because it was a sociable pastime, with lots of opportunity for sport.

Canadian soldiers at play in 1914

Two of his first recruits had been Frank Sherburn Hall and his brother Harry. The Colonel knew their father, as Mr Hall was the manager of his department store and a close neighbour. There was a training meeting once a week at the town's Armoury, with a chance for the men to fire their rifles.

Ex-sailor Frank enjoyed the comradeship at the Armoury, and he took to military routine quite naturally, as one might expect When they had a break from training, it was the practice to meet up for a meal at the nearby café. In this way Frank got to know the café's popular Chinese owner; Yip Foo.

Born in 1860, Yip Foo had travelled from his homeland as a young man to work on Canada's new railroad. In 1905 he settled in Moose Jaw, as one of the town's first Chinese immigrants. He was a devoted father of three children and became a member of the nearby Church.

Yip Foo

The outcome of Yip Foo's hard work and popularity was his success in local business. He was one of Alderman Herbert Snell's confidants. Mr Foo (as he was known by all) was later instrumental in helping Frank to find work after the war.

One of Frank's mates from the start was a cheerful Irish immigrant called Shaun. He was a married man with three children and worked locally as a logger. Despite, at 32 years, being much older than the average recruit, he was popular, and the men nicknamed him "Pops".

On the 1st of February 1915, Colonel Snell received an order to relinquish command of the 60th Rifles. He was instructed to immediately create and command a brand-new 600-man formation called the 46th Infantry Battalion. It was destined to be part of the Third Contingent of the Canadian Expeditionary Force (C.E.F.), destined for France. The unit's base was also at the Moose Jaw Armoury and recruitment was aimed at suitable men who lived locally. Frank Hall successfully transferred from the 60th Rifles a month after the new unit was formed. At that time Frank was still living at 112 Larch Avenue. He played baseball for his unit and was often invited after a game to dinner at Shaun's home, where he got to know the family. Shaun's wife Coleen was a good cook and her three young boys well-mannered and happy.

Intensive training began immediately to increase recruitment and to prepare the new unit for overseas service.

At a time when trained men were scarce, and leaders were urgently needed, Frank's background and experience caused him to stand out from the crowd. He was 27 and so a little older than most volunteers. (Just 7 years younger than his Colonel). Frank was fit, healthy, athletic, and from a good family. He had six months satisfactory service in the Militia plus his time in the Imperial Navy. In addition, he came from Yorkshire, not far from his Colonel's birthplace.

(It is likely that he failed to mention that he had deserted from the Navy after 8 years. It was quite a common occurrence in those days. In any

36

case, at the start of the war, the British Government issued a pardon to those ex-servicemen who had deserted in order that they could re-enlist, and their experience not be wasted).

He was an obvious choice for advancement, and consequently was promoted from Private soldier to Lieutenant within 5 months of his joining the new Battalion.

Because the attrition rate on the battlefields was enormous, newly formed units such as the 46th were repeatedly milked of manpower to provide reinforcements. Whole Companies of men were sent to bolster formations already deployed in Europe.

Several times Colonel Snell had to redouble his efforts to recruit and train yet more men to fill the gaps these drafts left. This turmoil delayed the 46th from joining the fight, and he and his men became very frustrated.

It was during this lull, on 24th April 1915, that Frank had his appendix removed at the Regina hospital. He made a favourable impression with the young nurses who were charmed at the influx of young soldier patients to care for.

Eventually on 26th May 1915, the big day arrived. Colonel Snell was ordered to entrain the 46th Battalion for Camp Sewell, a training cantonment in Manitoba.

(Built in 1909 Sewell had bell-tented accommodation and was designed to provide advanced training for troops prior to their being shipped to the front).

Members of the 46th Battalion C.E.F. entraining at Moose Jaw 1916

Two days later, a huge crowd consisting of families and townsfolk, complete with bands, assembled at the Moose Jaw rail station to see their men troop onto the waiting railcars.

At 0640 hrs promptly, with much cheering of goodwill from those on the platform, the train pulled out heading towards the east.

Before leaving Moose Jaw, Herbert Snell closed his business in preparation for his expected long absence overseas. This left William (Frank's father) out of work. However, armed with the Colonel's letters of reference and introduction, Mr Hall, at the age of 64, took this opportunity to move with his wife Annie across the border to Minnesota, USA.

There he found good employment as the buyer at a large department store in the city of Superior. His eldest son, Fred, moved at the same time from Nebraska to Duluth, on the banks of Lake Superior, to live near to his Mum and Dad.

__Superior city is on the western tip of Lake Superior, U.S.A.__

During the next five months at Camp Sewell the 46th were involved in more extensive training. Unfortunately, their instructors were mostly Boer War veterans, whose knowledge and experience of modern warfare was scant.

__Camp Sewell in Manitoba 1916__

South Saskatchewan recruitment was now being carried out by the 60th Rifles Militia unit back in Moose Jaw. The 46th Battalion's manpower was repeatedly and severely depleted, and its numbers built up again and again with newly enlisted, untrained men. Each time this happened, Colonel Snell and his officers had to train and integrate the newcomers before the Battalion could again be judged fit for overseas service. This caused huge irritation to the soldiers, and to their officers, who found it hard to bear. Frank was not included in any of the drafts that were sent ahead, and stayed with his Colonel, helping to train the ever-changing faces of the battalion. To increase their fitness and group bonding, regular sport was played, coupled with a weekly 20-mile route march, carrying full kit. They became increasingly proficient with their (Canadian) Ross rifles on the firing ranges.

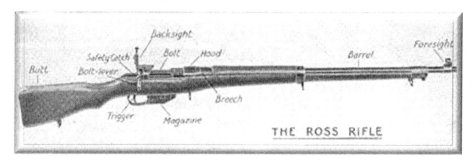

<u>46th Battalion soldiers training before being shipped to England</u>

Frank took this opportunity to fully equip himself with his officer's attire and equipment, which he had to buy with his own money. Included in his requirements were tailored jackets, collared shirts, and ties. A leather Sam Brown belt, with holster for his Colt .45 automatic pistol, completed the picture.

<u>Colt ·45 automatic pistol like the one that Frank carried</u>

With all of this going on, the active outdoor summer life in the countryside was not altogether disagreeable to the troops.

Eventually, and with just a week's notice, Colonel Snell and his officers were overjoyed to receive orders to entrain the whole 46th Battalion for overseas service. Their sister Battalion, the 44th was to travel from Sewell, with them.

The battalion's strength at that point was 36 officers and 1,115 other ranks. Although plans for a short-notice move had been made, the seven days were packed with activity for the men and their leaders. Their experiences in Camp Sewell had brought home to them the massive casualty rates suffered by British troops in France. Now the time had come to leave the safety of Canada. There were some desertions, but most of the men stayed, although they could not have failed to realise how precarious the future might be for them. A lot of letter-writing to mothers and sweet-hearts at home took place, before the men left the prairies.

The 18 Oct 1915 finally arrived, and they packed themselves and their equipment onto the immigrant cars which were coupled behind a huge C.P.R. locomotive.

Soon the two infantry battalions started their journey traversing the breadth of Eastern Canada. They settled down to their long crossing with the stoical patience that people, without smart phones or televisions, behaved in those days. They played cards (Crown and Anchor) told stories, sang songs, read books, talked to each other, and wrote letters and diaries. Their company cooks used the immigrant stoves to prepare their meals, and each evening their band entertained them with a musical concert. By this stage in the war, thousands of wartime Canadian songs had been written.

They expressed patriotism, national identity, sentimentality, and gender roles. Some of them were "The Best Flag on Earth" (1914), "I Love You Canada", "Khaki", and "I Want My Daddy". Shaun's harmonica renditions were very popular, and the units travelled in high spirits.

Popular music sung by the soldiers

At an average of 35 mph, the train had 3,700 miles to cover. After passing from Manitoba province into Ontario, they stopped to refuel at Winnipeg, on the Red River.

(This city is famed as the coldest winter city in the world. Two hundred years previously it had been a much-fought-over French, and then British (Hudson Bay Company), fur trading base. In 1811 families escaping the Highland Clearances in Scotland began farming there at the Red River, Selkirk Settlement. Their town, in time, developed into present day Winnipeg).

Stopping the next day at lonely MacPherson Station to take on water and fuel, the men strained at the carriage windows to catch a glimpse of the "enemy" as they steamed past an internment camp.

(Several civilian ships had been torpedoed and sunk in the Atlantic since the war had started. As a result, the Canadian government had opened civilian internment camps for "enemy/aliens", i.e., German/Canadians and conscientious objectors. These camps eventually held over 8,000 people).

The train passed Fort William and then Romford before, two days later, approaching the mighty French city of Montreal in Quebec Province.

After a brief stop for refuelling, they pulled away from the platform to pass small settlements with names which revealed the origins of the people who had settled there. They passed Farnham, Scotstown, and Somerset before pulling into St John to take on yet more logs and water. The men were keen customers to the eager children who vended snacks and cigarettes on the platform. Continuing on past Oxford, Londonderry, Truro, and Windsor Junction, eventually their train puffed into its final destination. They had now arrived at the ice-free Atlantic port of Halifax.

Halifax in Nova Scotia 1916

Had they continued along the coast for a further 200 miles they would have passed Liverpool and Yarmouth. (It was as if they were being prepared for their future in Britain).

Tied up at the quay, was a 2-funnelled passenger liner, the SS Lapland. Previously used to transport emigrants, she had been built in Belfast by Harland and Wolff eight years previously. Fitted with twin screws, and capable of reaching 17 knots, she was, for her day, fast. The weary men boarded her straight off the train and were allocated their accommodation. Some were lucky, but many were issued with hammocks, to be strung wherever there was space. They were to sail the next day.

Little did they know of the **Mont Blanc incident** which would occur there, two years later. *(On the morning of 6th December 1917, a French cargo named the SS Mont Blanc ship was moving slowly near to the Halifax docks. At 0845hrs it was involved in a collision with another cargo ship. The Mont Blanc was loaded with war explosives and motor spirit. The huge explosion that soon followed was, at that time, the biggest man-made detonation that had ever occurred in world history. It flattened a large section of Halifax, killing 2,000 people, including a nearby First Nation community (who were wiped out), and injured 9,000 more people. It caused a tsunami, and nearly all structures within a half mile radius were obliterated).*

A view of the damage on the 6th December 1917 at Halifax

That night the more thoughtful men talked quietly together about the RMS Lusitania. Five months previously this liner, full of passengers, sailed alone from New York on route for Liverpool. Launched in 1906 on the Clydebank she had been the fastest liner in the world. Eleven miles off the Irish coast she had been torpedoed by a German submarine and sank within 20 minutes. 1,200 people had drowned, including 216 Canadians. Many of them had been soldier's wives and children, enroute to be near to their men in England.

The 46th Battalion men woke early in the cold and dark of the next day pre-dawn. In poor weather SS Lapland slipped from the quayside, and maintaining radio silence, sailed for England.

SS Lapland

Steaming at her maximum speed, she travelled alone and unescorted, as had the Lusitania. Keeping clear of normal shipping lanes, the liner ploughed through heavy seas for several days and long nights. Many men suffered badly from seasickness throughout the journey.

To former sailor Frank, this was a familiar environment, and he did what he could to re-assure his men. With the other officers, he played his part in giving the men entertaining lectures in the various mess-decks. The band did their best to take the men's minds off the discomfort. They played them the sort of music that they thought would help. Shaun with his harmonica came to the fore.

Eventually on the sixth day, the crow's-nest look-out reported to the bridge that he had sighted two warships to the east. Several pairs of binoculars were quickly focussed onto the horizon. Gradually the blurred shapes materialized into two Royal Navy destroyers, sent out to escort the lone liner into safe harbour. As the warships closed with the SS Lapland the relieved Canadians lined the deck to spontaneously cheer the Royal Navy's arrival. Frank must have had feelings of poignancy as he stared across at the familiar ships and uniforms.

That evening Colonel Snell ordered Frank to give his men a briefing of what they should expect when they reached dry land. Amongst other information he imparted, he told them:

"*Soon we will reach England, and you will be disembarking at the famous port of Plymouth, a port that has long been associated with the voyages of pioneers and adventurers. For centuries emigrants have departed from there, to colonize countries (including Canada) around the world. One result of this is that there are now over 50 towns worldwide called by the same name as the port we will make tomorrow.*

It was from this base that, in 1577, Sir Francis Drake set off in the Golden Hind becoming the first person to circumnavigate the world.

Just 8 years after his return to England, Drake was second in command of the English fleet which sailed from our haven to successfully challenge the Spanish Armada.

<u>The Pilgrim Fathers set sail on the Mayflower in 1620</u>

<u>They left to establish a colony on the Massachusetts coast. (30 million people are now descendants of the 132 folk who took that journey)</u>

**_James Cook accompanied by naturalist Charles Darwin
set off in HMS Beagle in 1831._**

Both of James Cook's famous voyages (1788 and 1831) began from this small town. Cook was accompanied on his second voyage, by the naturalist, Charles Darwin.

It has been designated the main entry port for Empire troops assisting the Empire in this war.

The first Canadian troops arrived here last year, complete with a bear cub as their regimental mascot."

****

Chapter 7

Training at Bramshott Camp

On the next evening, SS Lapland was shepherded safely into Plymouth's natural harbour. As she steamed past the Hoe and Devil's Point the Canadians lined the decks and gasped at the huge Dreadnoughts and other grey-painted British warships moored around them.

__A Royal Navy Dreadnaught at anchor in Plymouth Sound 1916__

Soon, to the sounds of clanging bells, they manoeuvred up to the quayside inside the Devonport Naval base. There the SS Lapland moored up and the signal "stop engines" was passed from the bridge.

At last, a still silence settled over the ship. Arriving back in the familiar country of their birth, many of the soldiers must have had very nostalgic feelings.

There was no shore leave, and that night they were briefed to prepare for boarding a train for the next stage of their journey.

Early the next day, having eaten a good breakfast and prepared their equipment, all 2,000 troops filed down the gangplanks onto the quayside.

46th Battalion forming up after disembarking
from SS Lapland at Plymouth

There were no welcoming crowds, just the early morning bustle and noise of a busy dockyard. After forming into ranks of three, the Senior Warrant Officer marched them off a short distance to a railway siding where a passenger train waited. The men gasped with amusement to see it. By Canadian Pacific Railway standards, it looked like a toy.

Their 'toy train' took them all to Liphook

Soon after they were loaded, eight men to a compartment, a flag was waved. To the sound of steam escaping, the coal-fired engine started moving. With gathering speed, it pulled the train away from the station. Their odyssey continued.

__Beautiful English countryside, seen through the carriage windows.__
__Such a contrast to Saskatchewan's prairies__

The passengers soon saw that they were passing through very novel and unfamiliar countryside.

It was noticeable, compared with that which they had become used to, how quietly, smoothly, and rapidly their train covered the miles.

They gazed in wonderment through the windows, at southern England's countryside, in all its ever-changing late autumn beauty.

They flashed past small villages and tiny cottages. Little farms with hedged fields, passed in the blink of an eye.

*__Many of the men, were English born, and felt nostalgic
as they rattled across the countryside__*

They caught momentary sightings of country folk riding or driving horses and sheep along inexplicably winding, narrow, hedged lanes.

__The views brought back fond memories of their lives before Canada__

*For a split second they caught the frozen looks on faces,
and then they were gone*

It all looked so very peaceful and ordered. Suddenly, with a shattering roar, another train passed going in the opposite direction.

They remembered, with relief, that in England there are two tracks

Soon they settled down as they were used to passing the time, by reading, talking, and playing cards. Before long they discovered that there were no lavatories in the carriages. However, they were promptly shown by their 'British' friends, how to lower the windows!

After a journey that included several unexplained and lengthy stops, the 46th Battalion arrived on 22nd October 1915, at a small East Hampshire town, near to the border with Surrey. There, with their piles of equipment, they de-trained onto the short platform at 9.30 pm. They had arrived at Liphook. The men were exhausted and hungry, not having eaten for several hours.

Told to "Fall in", they were addressed by their Colonel. Almost apologetically, he told them that their camp was 3 miles away, and that there was a "muck-up". There was no transport available, and they would have to march to their new camp.

Their recent training had hardened them to facing challenges, and so they philosophically sorted themselves out for the journey. Equipment was split into manageable loads, and they set off. It was hard going, but eventually just before midnight the weary Battalion arrived at (North) Bramshott Camp. It consisted a few old wooden huts on a 1½ by 1-mile plot of undeveloped sandy soil. A skeleton staff were keeping watch over what had once been a camp for the British Army. The 46th were not expected and found that no provisions had been made for the arrival of their 1,200 men. It started to rain.

This situation put a huge strain on the officers, who were as tired as their men. After a brief conference, Colonel Snell sent his key men off to find transport. Commandeering local people's horses and bicycles, some of the officers set out straight away to the Canadian Army Headquarters at Aldershot, 15 miles to the north. Once there, they roused responsible officers and announced the Battalion's arrival at Bramshott. They had not been expected for another month.

Rapid arrangements were made to have sufficient tents, bedding and rations sent to Bramshott that night. Within a week, Pioneers brought and erected large, new, wooden huts. Proper kitchens with a steady supply of rations and other essentials were established. Local people, alerted to the issue, did what they could to help.

None-the-less, during the first few days a proportion of the 46th Battalion's men left the camp without authority. They went to find food and somewhere to sleep. Some of British origin who had friends and family living nearby, went to them. Some caught the next train to London, there to stay at the Union Jack Club. (Canadian soldiers received far more pay than did their British counterparts). British Military Police were alerted to find the missing men, and before long the absentees started to return.

Discipline problems continued with some of the troops who were, after all, civilians in uniform. Initially their conduct was wanting, with too much drunkenness, fighting, and absence without leave. A proportion of soldiers neglected to salute their officers or were otherwise insubordinate.

British Army instructors soon arrived, and the men were worked hard to reach the required standards.

Army routine was enforced, and penalties for offending military law included docked pay and detention. These young civilian/soldiers started their gradual transformation into properly trained soldiers, who accepted military law and were capable of fighting a war in France.

Within a few weeks the troops did settle down and liked their stay at Bramshott very much. This was helped by the very hospitable and welcoming attitude of the people who lived in the surrounding area. Frank, with the other officers, moved to a nearby pub which was requisitioned and used as the Officer's Mess.

It is a glowing reflection upon Colonel Snell's leadership that order was returned to his Battalion, so quickly. He was immensely proud of his Battalion's progress.

The young Colonel was however increasingly concerned about his wife and daughter. They had planned to cross the Atlantic to follow him to England. After several weeks he had no word from his wife Jessie. Very conscious that German U-boats were sinking passenger ships in the Atlantic, Herbert spent all his spare time writing to authorities trying to find out where his family was. Eventually, after three anxious weeks, he wrote to his bank who traced his wife to Liverpool, and they were reunited. Military regulations had forbidden a civilian from being told the location of any army unit! As more units arrived from Canada, Bramshott Camp rapidly grew to resemble a small town, measuring one by one and a half miles. By early May 1916 it was a well-appointed training camp.

Main Road through Bramshott Camp

There were sealed roads, which were lined with row upon row of wooden huts. Running water, kitchens, and a sewerage system were installed, as were ablutions, latrines, and showers. A gymnasium and a games ground were built, with nearby concert hall and open-air theatre. Several wet canteens were permitted and the local populace-built cinemas (3 pence a seat), cafes, and an array of shops lining the adjacent London to Portsmouth Road. This included a large building called "Funland", which had a miniature rifle range, a "slot" organ, two billiard tables and a three-penny cinema. The Salvation Army and the YMCA (Young Men's Christian Association) set up soldiers' huts and canteens to "entertain the mind, spirit and body". There, in a non-alcohol environment, they held religious ceremonies and encouraged the men to socialise, play cards, write letters, and perform shows.

Other huts were transformed into churches, and on Sundays, tea and coffee was sold there at 1 penny a cup, and cake at 2 pennies a slice.

The Royal Anchor pub, Liphook

A weekly camp magazine called The Bramshott Souvenir Magazine containing jest, cartoons, and verse, was created. Ex-journalist soldiers doubled as reporters. Sporting events and dances were a regular occurrence. Civilians from the nearby towns of Haslemere, Liphook, Grayshott, and Hindhead rallied round to help the soldiers settle in. Some lonely soldiers were able to accept invitations to spend time at the homes of local people. The townsfolk in turn attended dances and came to watch sports events when invited. The Royal Anchor pub in Liphook became very popular with the men.

Local authorities, alerted by the number of romances between soldiers and local girls, reduced the cost of a marriage licence to a fifth of what it had previously been.

Training and Army activities rapidly intensified as news from the front informed of the horrific casualty rates. Nearby Witley Camp was created to provide specialist instruction, and a Canadian military hospital came into being on the east side of the A3 road.

At Bramshott the soldiers were taught the skills of bombing, bayonet-fighting, entrenching, and wiring. Signalling training was carried out at Liphook's Highfield School.

It was felt vital that the training included instructional lessons on health matters. During the whole war, figures show that 15.8% of Canadian troops suffered from a venereal disease. This was six times the rate of British troops, and so there developed a series of lectures warning the men about the dangers of 'immoral women'.

Despite the scary haranguing from the medics and the busy training activity, there were many war babies from liaisons between the young men from Saskatchewan and local women.

The battalion's Canadian high-collared uniforms and some of their equipment were found to be unsuitable and the men were issued with British uniforms and equipment. They did retain a maple leaf "Canada" and "Overseas Service" badges. (Symbols which they wore, with great pride).

They choose to emulate their British counterparts by allowing their facial hair to grow. Big bushy moustaches, called "Old Bills", or Charlie Chaplin styles were common. (Anything for a laugh!)

__Charlie Chaplin was a very popular entertainer in 1916__

To mark their individuality, the Canadians removed the wire stiffeners from their issued peaked caps, but eventually took a preference to the (British) trench cap (called a "Cor Blimy") with its warm ear flaps.

Garbed further in collarless grey flannel shirts, and khaki trousers held up to the belly button by stout braces, they started to look the part. British hob-nailed boots, a pair of puttees, a great-coat, two blankets, a razor with shaving brush, tooth, hair and boot brushes, water bottle, mess tins, rifle oil bottle, pull-through, and bayonet with scabbard all added to the picture.

All troops were issued steel helmets. As a Lieutenant, Frank was responsible for buying his own uniform.

Eventually, with the Infantry added to the Artillery, Cavalry and the Army Service Corps units, there were over 20,000 soldiers based at Bramshott and nearby Witley camps combined.

As a 2nd Lieutenant in a British infantry battalion, the famous poet, 23-year-old Wilfred Owen, was at Witley Camp at that time. He was recovering there from shell shock. To while away his time there, he penned a prelude to his famous anti-war poem "Anthem for Doomed Youth". One wonders what the effect on the Canadians would have been had they met him at that stage of the war. Owens was killed in action two years later.

__Wilfred Owen in 1916__

Violet lived at home in Haslemere. For several days each week she helped with secretarial work at her father's yard, at Funnell and Furlonger's in the nearby village of Grayshott.

It is at this stage of the story that Violet met Frank. As a pretty, 23-year-old she was quite naturally attracted by the flood of young men with unusual accents moving into the area. When invited to the camp dances or sporting events, she happily went there with her friends. By this time Lieutenant Frank Hall (aged 26) was the Signals Officer of his battalion. He was chosen for this role partly because he had been a Navy signalman, four years previously. Such experience was hard to find on the Canadian prairies. He was also an accomplished sportsman and had been very keen on physical activity since he had been a child. He and Violet met each other at a baseball match in Bramshott Camp in the spring of 1916. Frank was self-assured and good looking. There was a mutual attraction and Violet's friendship with Frank progressed rapidly.

Violet (middle) with friends watching the Canadians soldiers playing baseball in 1916

Before long, Frank laid an army telephone line from his work-hut at Bramshott Camp to her home in Grayshott. This was 1½ miles away and done (without any authority) so that he and she could regularly speak to each other.

__Frank was very familiar with the field telephones then in use__

As Violet and Frank talked and their friendship grew, they found that they had a lot in common. Both benefited from being brought up in respectable, comfortably-off families.

__A foot operated Singer sewing machine, in common usage in 1916__

Violet had trained as a dressmaker and was first class at her trade. She specialised in hand-making elaborate, expensive wedding dresses for wealthy people in Haslemere and sometimes further afield. Violet made these dresses at home using the Singer sewing machine that her parents had bought her. Having worked in his father's drapery business, Frank appreciated and was impressed by the skills that she possessed. Violet helped Frank to turn out as smartly as possible, by tailoring his uniforms, and sewing on his badges.

Violet would surely have told Frank about her nightly knitting of warm clothing for her cousins serving in France. (I wonder who the wool that I found in her loft all those years later was destined for?) And she must have told Frank of her brother Walter, who was also a soldier.

The men's training continued and concentrated on musketry, grenade-throwing, drill, and manoeuvring on a battlefield. These keen, confident young men made rapid progress. The standards of preparedness for war were reached on 26th April 1916. Colonel Snell's Battalion was thrilled to be allocated as a component unit in the newly formed 4th Canadian Division, which had just been alerted for active service. The 46th was to join the 44th Battalion (Manitoba), the 47th Battalion (British Columbia), and the 50th Battalion (Alberta), as part of the 10th Brigade of that Division. That evening they proudly went out for a drink to celebrate.

A Canadian infantry battalion consisted of approximately 1,000 men plus some extras. In addition to the Headquarters staff, the battalion had four companies. In each company were four platoons, and each platoon had four sections. The Colonel also had at his disposal, a machine gun section, a scout/sniper section, a grenade section, a signals section, a transport section, and the stretcher bearers (the band). Each man needed training in his specialist skills

While they were poised to leave for the front, other Canadian units who were already fighting in France were suffering an appalling rate of casualties.

Newer units were consequently subject to continual cannibalization as reinforcements to make up the casualties at the front. In early June Colonel Snell was ordered to send 800 of his men, to make up these depletions. He was to receive fresh new recruits straight from Canada. The Colonel was devastated and faced with completely rebuilding the identity and training standard of his battalion.

This style of disruption happened to all the Canadian Expeditionary Force (CEF) infantry battalions. It was a constant throughout the war. As a result, just 48 of the 258 Canadian infantry battalions that were created, fought as an entity. The rest were split up to be used as casualty replacements. (At that time Canada had a population of just 8 million people, and the CEF needed, 80,000 soldiers each year just to make up the numbers. They were forced eventually to follow the British practice of legislating for conscription.) Before long Bramshott Camp was, in part, a reinforcement depot.

Frank wasn't one of those soldiers sent to France as a reinforcement. It is likely that Colonel Snell needed him to help in future training, and that there was no-one else available to fill the important role of Signals Officer.

Two weeks later Colonel Snell was watching some of his men in a trench, practicing throwing Mills bombs. The instruction was carried out by British Army trainers, and was a fairly simple skill, but very dangerous if done incorrectly.

The bomb was held in the throwers hand in a live condition and would detonate four seconds after being released. Upon explosion, potentially lethal metal fragments would fly out in all directions. On the day that Colonel Snell chose to watch the training, a nervous young soldier fumbled and dropped his grenade. Six other soldiers, including the sergeant instructor were close by. Col Snell was the first to react and he attempted to throw the bomb over the parapet before it went off. However, it detonated before he could accomplish that. The fumbler and the Sergeant instructor were killed immediately, and two other soldiers and Herbert Snell were very badly hurt. Amongst other injuries, he lost an eye. The Colonel was rushed to the nearby hospital and was not expected to live.

Another officer (Colonel Dawson) was appointed to command the battalion, and the induction and training of new men continued apace. More and more soldiers were arriving from Canada.

A Mills hand grenade of the type that the soldiers trained to use

One of the recent reinforcement soldiers sent from the barracks in Moose Jaw was Private Harry Corrigan. He was a 27-year-old mechanic who had been a neighbour and friend of Frank's in Moose Jaw. He had also been one of his companions in the 60th Rifles, and now Harry was one of the 46th Battalion at Bramshott.

On the 18thJune, Frank was admitted to Bramshott hospital for a few days suffering from a strained back. This was due to the athletics injury that had occurred during his schooldays.

Violet came to see him every day, and one day as they talked and held hands Frank realised how much he would miss his girl and how much he loved her. Neither could imagine being without the other. Frank was 28 years old and Violet just 23.

The next day when she visited, Violet was surprised to see that they were alone in the ward. Frank took Violet's hands into his and looked her straight in the eyes, saying, "Vi I am going to France soon and I don't know what the future holds, but I want us to share our lives together. I love you, and always will, with all my heart. Please marry me".

Violet cool-headedly considered the words that she had been expecting for some time. She knew that the future was uncertain, but she felt to her core that he was a good man. Her heart was beating fast, and she knew that she loved Frank very much.

Frank looked at her intently whilst she considered what and how to reply. It was all happening so fast, but that is often what happens in the urgency of war. It only took a few seconds for her to decide, and she replied, "Thank you for asking me Frank dearest, I would be honoured to be your wife." They smiled at each other and kissed with mingled tears running down their cheeks. Almost as an afterthought Violet added, "Oh, you had better ask my father". The ward nurses, who had been in on Frank's plan, then came smiling back into the room to congratulate them.

Canada's Dominion Day falls on 1st July each year. This joyous occasion is celebrated by Canadians the world over commemorating their country's 1879 Confederation. On that special day in 1916, along a 15-mile front of the Somme River area of France, thousands of allied soldiers waited tensely, in soggy trenches, for the screech of their officer's whistles. Their artillery had performed a massive bombardment over the whole of the past week.

This was intended to annihilate any possible opposition to the allied attack. The men were primed for an easy victory. At 0730 hrs, as ordered, they dutifully scrambled over the parapets and walked purposefully towards the German lines.

Advancing spaced apart, the attackers were amazed to encounter intact barbed wire, and then a fierce, effective resistance from their enemy. The bulk of the Germans had survived the shelling, and were defending their deep dugouts, armed with hundreds of machine guns, firing on fixed lines. Aided by their massed artillery, they mowed the advancing infantry down and within minutes had inflicted thousands of casualties.

On that first day 19,240 Allied soldiers died

There was an average of about one killed every five seconds. To take one case in point, the (Canadian) Newfoundland Regiment was almost completely, annihilated. It lost 732 of its 800 men.

The Battle of the Somme lasted for another 5 months and proved to be one of history's bloodiest conflicts. There were 1,123,907 allied casualties for an average 5 miles of advance.

At 10 a.m. on the day that the battle began, whilst the Somme landscape was erupting just 150 miles away, there was a huge pageant at Bramshott Camp. The Canadian 4th Division's fresh infantry troops were mustered on the camps parade ground. Violet was one of the hundreds of invited spectators to watch the 46th Battalion at the ceremony. To the sounds of bands playing and with their chests swelling with pride, Frank and his compatriots were reviewed by the King of Britain, George V. Their date with destiny was fast approaching.

Five weeks later the 46th Battalion, was again given warning of their imminent transfer to France.

****

Chapter 8

Band of Brothers into Battle

On Thursday, the 10thAugust 1916, in high spirits and led by their band, the 46th Battalion left Bramshott camp. The young men marched off with an ostentatious swank, cheerfully singing the familiar music hall songs of the time. Local people lined the route into Liphook, to wish this latest south-heading battalion the very-best of luck. The girls blew kisses whilst small boys ran alongside the columns in excitement. The adults watched the men with a knowing disquietude. Violet sobbed quietly as she watched her dear husband-to-be, march off at the head of his men. She felt wretched.

Good-bye-ee, Good-by-ee!
Wipe the tear baby dear, from your eye-ee
Tho' it's hard to part, I know,
I'll be tickled to death to go.
Don't cry-ee---don't sigh-ee!
There's a silver lining in the sky-ee!
Bon-soir old thing! Cheer-i-o! chin-chin!
Na-poo! Too-dle-oo! Good-bye-ee

After reaching Liphook and then swinging right, the men were halted at the railway station, where they boarded a special troop-train. Soon they set off for Southampton docks. Gazing out of the windows at the peaceful and by now familiar Hampshire countryside, the young soldiers became strangely quiet. As they approached Rowlands Castle the engineer pulled a cord and a loud whistle alerted people on the platform that the train would flash through. Some of the troops wondered if they would ever see this land again. So much had happened and they had learned so much since steaming from Halifax. They had spoken with veterans returned from France, and they knew of the conditions and of the horrendous casualty rates. They had heard about gas and seen the gruesome results of shell warfare. Their immediate future was one of a precarious existence, in the cold, the wet and in the mud. What they faced, as individual infantry soldiers, was very real danger to their lives. No longer did it seem like a jolly adventure, but all the same they were proud to go. Honoured to fight for Britain. Soon after the train arrived at the Southampton dockyard, the men trooped to the wharf and then straight up the gangway onto the 20-year-old Belgium ferry, Princess Clementine.

**Belgian Paddle Steamer, Princess Clementine with a top speed of 22 knots was used as a troop carrier and could carry 1,000 soldiers**

As the sun rose the next morning, their ship started moving slowly from the dock. Once out of the harbour, the 324-foot, three-decked vessel rapidly accelerated. Her twin side wheels moved the paddles into a splashing blur of rhythmic motion. At its top speed of 22 knots, the small ship gained through a choppy sea, into the English Channel, on a direct course for the French coast. The captain on the bridge, very aware of the threat from enemy submarines, mines and torpedo boats had carefully briefed and posted his lookouts. After a short crossing, the ship tied up at the wharf in the port of Le Havre. Once disembarked, the men were marched off to follow a well-trodden path. Soon they were directed to climb into rail waggons marked "*Quatre chavaux ou dix hommes*" (four horses or ten men), then they rattled off on the next stage of the journey. Half an hour later they pulled up beside a group of warehouses. There they jumped off the freight trucks to be met by cheerful Army cooks who served them their first meal of the day.

__Soldiers were generally well fed with wholesome, if basic food__

Higher Command had decided that this raw battalion would benefit by spending a week in a relatively quiet sector of the Ypres salient in Belgium. This was to be in a section of the front line with the experienced Imperial (British) 2nd Division. Only after this induction could they be judged sufficiently prepared to take on the responsibility of a more dangerous sector. Within an hour they entrained again.

The last 33 miles of their long peregrination, however, was done on foot, in the cold rain, carrying full kit.

It was important to take care of your feet!

They were issued with no rations, and so at ten p.m., when they finally arrived at their destination, the exhausted men ate their evening meal ravenously.

That over, the half-asleep soldiers were directed to some soft hay in nearby ramshackle barns. Frank and his fellow officers were shown to billets in the farmhouses.

An introduction to life in the trenches

During the next week, the battalion was introduced to life in the trenches. They became accustomed to the frequent and dangerously unpredictable explosions.

They got used to the ever-present sniper and machine gun fire. They took part in patrols into no-man's-land. There was the occasional casualty, and one man was killed by shellfire. Their new, very firm, Colonel quickly earned the battalion's respect, and they became inured to sharing their soggy trenches with an infestation of rats and lice. By 20thAugust their initiation was complete, and Frank's friend Harry Corrigan had been promoted to Corporal. The 46th made ready for their next stage of modern warfare.

One day, soon after Frank had gone to war, Violet left her home in Haslemere to measure-up a customer in Liphook for a wedding dress. On the way there, she called in at the town's Post Office to send off some of her regular parcels of knitted woollens. The newly arrived Postmaster's wife who served her looked at the details on the rear of Violet's packages, and recognised the name Furlonger. After a few rapid questions, the two women realized that they knew each other.

The Postmistress was called Flora Thompson, and fifteen years previously had worked in the nearby village of Grayshott. She had been the assistant Post Mistress and telegraph machine operator, and in her employment she had become familiar with the local businesses and with the celebrities who called at the Post Office. Flora certainly remembered the Grayshott transport company of Funnel and Furlongers. She liked children, and easily remembered the pretty eight-year-old Violet Furlonger who happily ran messages for her father.

Flora Thompson in 1921

These two women were delighted to meet up again. They arranged to get together for tea later that week when Flora's children would be at school.

Flora had noticed and was curious that one of the packages had been addressed to a Canadian soldier. Over tea she asked Violet who the packages were for. This prompted Violet to tell Flora all about her knitting, and her "young man" who was with the Canadian Army in France. After she had received this information, Flora countered by telling Violet of her own dear brother Edwin. He had been a Boer War soldier who had emigrated to Canada in 1911. At the outbreak of war, Edwin had enlisted into the Canadian Army. After a transfer in early 1916 to the 2nd Battalion as a casualty replacement, he had been sent to Belgium. What the Postmaster's wife didn't tell Violet on that occasion was that Edwin had been killed at Ypres four months previously. It was too raw for her, and in any case she didn't wish to upset Violet.

Flora changed the subject and reminisced about her life in Grayshott, of her role there and of the people she had known.

(When Violet had been 17, her parents had a lodger called Garnett Boniface who was employed at the Haslemere Post Office as a telegraphist. So Violet was familiar with the telegraph operating aspect of Flora's work).

When the London to Portsmouth railway line had been constructed, the new accessibility had attracted a lot of intellectuals to leave smoky London and live locally for the benefit of their health. During Flora's time in Grayshott this clique had included writers Arthur Conan Doyle, his friend and neighbour Grant Allen (a Canadian), the author Richard Le Gallienne and George Bernard Shaw. Flora had got to know them quite well because they called regularly at the Post Office to send telegrams and post letters.

The older woman explained that her association with these successful men of letters had greatly interested her but had daunted her own serious writing ambitions.

She did have what today would be thought of as feminist emancipation convictions, which were fashionable in those days. She was impressed that Violet was a strong-minded young woman, who had started her own successful business. Flora liked that her new friend had done this by her own independent efforts. She had always appreciated fashionable clothing and found herself admiring the quality of Violet's up-to-date and well-made attire.

Although Flora was by nature a loner, and some 15 years the senior, the two women's friendship blossomed, and they enjoyed talking together. Violet determined to introduce Flora to her Frank when he came on leave.

In mid-August, Frank's battalion was transferred from Belgium to the area of the River Somme in France. The army was maximising its strength there in preparation for an imminent attack on the Germans. The 46th battalion had a further short attachment to another seasoned unit. (This spell included a gas exposure exercise). After that they were considered ready to re-join the Canadian 4th Division and assigned to their own sector of the front line.

One of the most hazardous jobs that a young infantry officer could be assigned to, was that of a platoon commander. The need to set an example and lead in action caused this function to be amongst the most perilous positions to be in. As the battalion's Signals Officer, Lieutenant Hall would have been worked hard doing a technical and dangerous job. However, it would not have been quite as risky a role as it was for some of his fellow officers.

It was a very dangerous life for a junior infantry officer

Frank's duties would have been vital to his Colonel. As the Commanding Officer of the battalion, it was essential that he had a reliable and immediate means of contact with his Brigadier.

At the same time, it was imperative that he could pass and receive messages, in the heat of a battle and at other times, to and from all his battalion's dispersed units. He had to be in touch with adjoining infantry, artillery, medical, supply, and flying corps components of the Army.

Frank had a lot of responsibility, the bare minimum of trained men at his disposal and not a lot of personal rank. His section's main preoccupation would have been the laying and maintaining of telegraph wires from unit to unit across the front.

In addition, they cut German wires and/or intercepted their messages. Not least of his responsibilities would have been to provide runners to pass urgent messages across the field of conflict. This would have been very hazardous work, especially during a battle.

His men would have become proficient in the use of electrical telegraph systems (cutting edge technology at that time) morse code, flag signal telegraph, and carrier pigeons.

A Signallers role often left them very exposed

Some messages would have best been sent by motor vehicle or by a horse-rider. Fragile equipment and important logbooks would have to be kept safe and dry in atrocious conditions, and Frank would have been on call 24 hours a day. He had a batman assigned to him in order that he could apply his time and energy to achieving his function.

Unarmed stretcher bearers risked their lives to save others as a matter of course and earned huge respect from their fellows for doing so

On many occasions men under Frank's command became casualties, often in the dangerous area of no-man's-land. Frank felt it his duty to do all that he could to bring his injured men back to safety. This often involved using the services of the unit's stretcher-bearers.

By this time his old friend Shaun had been promoted to Lance Corporal and had under his command a small section of the battalion's band as his stretcher bearer team.

Shaun earned Frank's admiration and gratitude night after night by risking his life in appallingly dangerous circumstances to bring men in. He was very popular and was often found leading trench singing and with his harmonica, bringing some cheer to his younger mates when the going was tough. It was often tough.

Break of day in the trenches (Isaac Rosenberg)

The darkness crumbles away.
It is the same old druid Time as ever,
Only a live thing leaps my hand,
A queer sardonic rat,
As I pull the parapet's poppy
To stick behind my ear.
Droll rat, they would shoot you if they knew
Your cosmopolitan sympathies.
Now you have touched this English hand
You will do the same to a German
Soon, no doubt, it will be your pleasure
To cross the sleeping green between.
It seems you inwardly grin as you pass
Strong eyes, fine limbs, haughty athletes,
Less chanced than you for life,
Bonds to the whims of murder,
Sprawled in the bowels of the earth,
The torn fields of France.
What do you see in our eyes
At the shrieking iron and flame
Hurled through still heavens?
What quaver — what heart aghast?
Poppies whose roots are in man's veins
Drop, and are ever dropping;
But mine in my ear is safe—
Just a little white with the dust.

An infantry battalion's routine on the Western Front had evolved into a distinct pattern over each 18-day period. They spent 6 days on the front line, 6 days in the reserve, followed by 6 days in support trenches.

By mid-September 1916, the 46th had completed two stretches "up the line". They became conditioned to living in constantly cold conditions. In rain and the consequential thick deep mire.

In unsanitary dangerous conditions, where rats and the cold, and wet were your constant companions, it was important to have someone keep up the troops' morale

They learned to accept as routine the exhausting night-time work parties, sentry duties and dangerous deep penetration patrols into no-man's land. Frank and his fellows experienced the terrifying trench mortar's nightly bombing when the enemy sought to pierce the Canadian's confined trenches. Just one success and several of Frank's men would be blown apart.

Constant tiredness taught the ability to fall asleep in seconds. Roused suddenly, they could operate effectively without the slightest hesitation. Daily rifle and foot inspections, breakfast of tea, bacon, and bread prepared by their own cooks after first light stand-to, became routine. They developed a protective insensitivity to the ever-present threat of death and injury. A sense of dark humour evolved which cast danger and discomfort into a hilarious if macabre joke.

Without the support and friendship of your mates life was tough

Very quickly they realised that the odds were stacked against them staying alive for very long. It wasn't so much a skill, that kept them alive, but luck. The term 'copped a Blighty one' was a common expression that they used in their conversations. It was a reference to those of their comrades who received an injury that caused them to be sent back to England. Preferably to stay there. Men in a combat situation saw that a life with scars was better than being permanently dead.

MATEY

Not comin' back to-night, matey,
And reliefs are comin' through,
We're all goin' out all right, matey,
Only we're leavin' you.
Gawd! It's a bloody sin, matey,
We go when reliefs come in, matey,
But you're stayin' 'ere to-night.
Over the top is cold, matey—
You lie on the field alone,

Didn't I love you of old, matey,
Dearer than the blood of my own
You were my dearest chum, matey—
(Gawd! but your face is white)
But now, though the reliefs 'ave come, matey,
I'm going alone tonight.
I'd sooner the bullet was mine, matey—
Goin' out on my own,
Leavin' you 'ere in the line, matey,
All by yourself, alone.
Chum o' mine and you're dead, matey,
And this is the way we part,
The bullet went through your head, matey,
But Gawd! It went through my 'eart.

....

The soldiers saw that their time in Belgium had been child's play in comparison with the real thing. Every morning they looked forward with happy anticipation to their large, issued tot of rum. This was given out under the supervision of young subalterns, like Frank.

The rum ration became an indispensable to these men

Since the soldiers had joined up, their reluctant companion had been their unreliable issued Ross rifles. Canadian politicians had insisted that Canadian soldiers used Canadian rifles. However, it was found that they were not suitable for trench warfare. An increasing number of Canadians, upon finding a discarded British Lee Enfield rifle, took it up to use in place of their issued weapon. (Both types of rifle used the same ammunition).

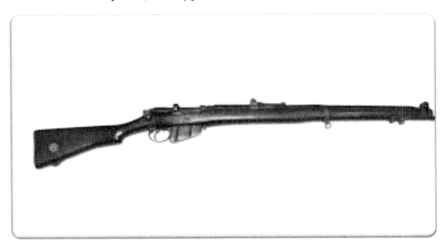

**_The British Lee Enfield rifle operated very well
in the wet, muddy conditions_**

Eventually during September 1916, the official decision was made, and all Ross rifles were replaced. On 18th September they trained in the use of their new Lee Enfield rifles at the nearby St Omer ranges.

(The discarded Ross rifles were next issued at the start of WW2. Due to the lack of other available small arms, they were used by the British Home Guard).

During the four weeks from 21st September 1916, the 46th Battalion fought on the Somme in a battle known as Regina Trench. They suffered an incredibly high level of casualties whilst fighting there. Most of the losses were due to machine gun fire, to gas and to shelling. Frank was faced with the fact that the bulk of his battalion's junior officers had been killed or wounded. To lose dear friends so suddenly and brutally hurt him to the core and he felt a need to keep an emotional distance from their replacements.

When Frank's own soldiers were killed it was his duty to collect their personal possessions and return them to the man's wife or next of kin. This was accompanied by a handwritten letter of condolence. Frank found that he often had to make more presentable the details and manner of the death. To tell a mother the stark, true details was more than he (or many of his contemporaries) would do. As time progressed, he found that sending off these letters became so frequent that he kept a standard wording in his little leather stationary case. He altered certain words dependent upon the circumstances, to provide some comfort for the recipient. In effect, he tried to sanitize the men's brutal ending, and he was quite unwilling to write down some of the accounts that he knew to be the facts. Stretcher bearers such as Shaun saw far more of this aspect of trench warfare than did most men.

An indication of the conditions endured by the 46th Battalion is shown in a letter sent by one of its men to his friend's mother in Moose Jaw:

Somewhere in Hell

26th October 1917

"Dear Mrs. ....

Just a note of sympathy from me and the old 46th Boys. I was talking to Harry yesterday morning and at 11am he was killed. He never suffered for a minute and was killed instantly. I have been here on active service for 16 months but the last few days beats all. I almost envy poor old Harry. It may be my turn before this note reaches you for, we are in the midst of death day and night and no letter of mine could give you any idea of what we are going through. I can't write a letter; my nerves are pitched too high. I trust it will relieve your mind to know a Moose Jaw boy saw your dear son and can assure you he suffered no pain. I hate to write and tell you but thought I would. If you call on Mrs R.L.Slater she will let you know who I am. You know me well yourself. Harry was killed 100 yards from me. Be brave Mrs. .... for your son died for the right and did his duty nobly but it's a poor consolation to you. My sympathy to you and all the family.

Yours very sincerely ...."

* * * * * * * * * * * * * * * * * * * *

It wasn't just skill, that kept men alive, but largely luck. Frank did everything he could to harden his emotions and decided that he would increase his prospects of survival by becoming as professional in his role as he could manage to be.

As the winter began, the weather became very cold and wet with a lot of snow. It stayed like that for months, and the troops found living for long periods in such muddy circumstances very trying. Influenza was rife and many men suffered from "trench foot" (a severe infection common in such conditions).

It was a relief when their turn came for a rotation out of the line into a support area. The battalion's vacancies due to casualty losses and illness were then filled with freshly trained soldiers from Bramshott Camp and with recovered wounded men.

Since Frank had arrived from England, he and Violet had corresponded lovingly and regularly. She had sent Frank a steady supply of her parcels and he and his men very much appreciated the warm woollens that supplemented their uniform wear.

Woollens sent by the men's womenfold were much appreciated

A large part of the role in support was manning fatigue parties (i.e. digging trenches and other fortifications, guarding prisoners, moving supplies, and repairing roads). There was, however, still a considerable danger of suffering from casualties due to shelling.

Soon they were sent to the reserve. Being further behind the front they were in less danger but did a lot of training (and catching up on sleep).

The men had to be prepared to reinforce the units on the front in case of any attack. They often lived in tents, but had access to hot baths and laundry facilities (improvised by the Engineers), regular hot food, and nearby civilian shops and pubs.

__Each reserve centre attracted large numbers of French prostitutes__

Very aware of the danger to the men's health, the military authorities arranged frequent lectures warning against the obvious dangers. Despite this, a few men tried to become deliberately infected to avoid a return to the front line. One can perhaps presume that they were, at best, unaware that the illness that they sought was generally incurable and that they risked one day dying of insanity.

In official recognition that morale was vital to any unit's ability to sustain the hardships, recreation was considered a vital part of life in the reserve. Film-shows, the YMCA (Young Men's Christion Association) and other church and voluntary civilian organisations played a large part in this. (Religion played an important part in the life of Canadians of that generation).

In the days before television, it was the practice within families and communities, to self-entertain themselves with music, song, jokes, and stories. A few men had worked on the stage, more played a musical instrument, whilst others had talents that they had learnt or were natural to them. Thus, it evolved that British soldiers themselves, all over the Western

Front, increasingly amused and delighted their fellows with self-produced concert shows. Irreverence to authority was a frequent theme, but the most popular of the performing troupes was the 3rd Division's "The Dumbells" (the name of which indicates the humorous appearance of men playing the part of dancing girls). The 4th Division's equivalent was, "The Maple Leaves".

Aware of the deteriorating morale of the French army, the British Military authorities wisely encouraged the entertainment, which they realised did a lot more good than it did harm.

"Well, if you knows of a better 'ole, go to it!"
Soldier/cartoonist Bruce Bairnsfather's best known work

An example of gallows humour that became common was an anecdote, passed to me in 2021 by a soldier's Grandson:

"They were a well bonded platoon, but one recent reinforcement was a loudmouth. He liked to boast, and this irritated his long-suffering fellows. It seemed to them that he always had his mouth open. One night in the trenches, they were shelled relentlessly. Each nearby explosion could so easily have been the one that would blow them apart. The men were half deafened and tried hard to hide the fact that they were very frightened, for hours. After a long time, there was a lull in the bombardment. In the quietness, their hearing began to readjust, and the men heard 'Loudmouths' panicky, slurred shouting, – I've been wounded! – They turned to him and saw that he had been hit by shrapnel in the mouth. In one cheek and out the other, missing his teeth completely

as his mouth had been wide open.

The platoon's reaction was to be immediately convulsed with maniacal laughter at the aptness of 'Loudmouth's Blighty One!' Only then were the stretcher bearers called for.

Before public radio, news was passed around by newspapers and periodicals. It developed that humour was the medium best appreciated by the troops. In reserve, Frank's normal workload was reduced and so it was decreed that Signals Officers should apply their spare energies to the battalion's recreation needs. Publications were produced and circulated by Signals Officers amongst the troops in the field. They were illustrated by a developing style of cartoon that matched the ordinary soldier's weary, droll sense of jocularity. This aspect of military life was very much enjoyed by the troops.

As part of this role, one day Frank went to a refreshment hut for soldiers at St Denis (near Paris). There he had to do a double take when he saw a uniformed 20-year-old girl who bore a striking resemblance to his fiancée Violet.

Betty Stevenson in 1917

81

The girl was much younger than most women who worked for the YMCA, had a vivacious personality and was obviously very popular. Frank made some enquiries before introducing himself to the girl.

***Betty Stevenson entertaining soldiers
in a Y.M.C.A. canteen in France***

This officer was a handsome confident young man and the two of them bonded immediately. Over cups of tea, he learned something about her. She had been born in the town of York (in Yorkshire), just 20 miles from Goole where Frank had been brought up. To his amazement she followed that information up by telling him that she had been schooled in Haslemere (where Violet was living). After finishing his tea Frank left, but they both knew that they had each made a new friend. The two of them met up for a chat whenever Frank's duties took him to St Denis. In that way he got to know Betty Stevenson.

Frank continued to take an interest in his friend, the stretcher bearer Shaun, who he had been in the Militia with. Frank also met up with his old Moose Jaw neighbour Harry Corrigan, who had been given early promotion to the rank of Sergeant.

On 27th January 1917, Frank was sent locally to attend an advanced Signaller's Course. There amongst many other skills, he learnt the cutting-edge technique of ground-to-aircraft radio communication. Ten days later he was posted to become a signals officer attached to the 4th Divisional Headquarters Signals Company. This new role involved doing a similar job to that which he did in the battalion, but well behind the front line. He took with him, his faithful batman.

Frank was one of several Lieutenants working under the command of a Royal Canadian Engineers Captain. The Signals Company was responsible for the whole division's communication systems.

During this time Frank helped to arrange for his pal Shaun, to transfer to the Divisional headquarters medical team (a safer job). Soon after his arrival, Shaun was promoted to Corporal and sent on a course to qualify as a medial orderly.

Frank was now involved in a lot of travelling around the Divisional area, and to help him do this, he was issued with a horse and assigned a groom to care for her. It wasn't long before Frank realized that his horse was very special. He soon became extremely fond of her. He named her Betty.

As each new technological development was introduced, fresh solutions to counter them had to be found. This applied for example when the enemy started using a tempered steel wire in the cables used for sending their telegraph messages. This proved extremely difficult to cut with normal equipment.

During early April 1917 the Canadian 4th Division was involved in a short but vicious battle called Vimy Ridge. The Canadian front-line units suffered horrendous casualties, and Frank was very fortunate to be now mostly employed some distance from the fighting.

Then at the end of May 1917, the Division moved its location from France to Belgium. They were located in a marshy area of Flanders, near to the city of Ypres.

A month after the relocation, Frank had been on continuous active service for 9 months and he applied for UK leave. This was granted from Saturday 23rd June 1917, for a ten-day period. He caught the very next transport to Le Havre and there boarded the leave boat. Arriving at Southampton he bundled himself and his bag straight onto the waiting Haslemere train and was with Violet later the same day.

These two had first met 14 months before but had spent 10 months of that apart. In common with many women in those times of uncertainty, Violet had obtained a special marriage licence prior to Frank's arrival. She had everything arranged, and two days after his leave began Violet and Frank were married in the Church of St. Peters in the ancient Surrey Hills village of Hambledon. This is close to Chiddingfold and in an area where many of Violet's relatives lived. It was a hot sunny day but there was a hint of thunder clouds on the horizon.

St Peters Church, Hambledon

The reception was packed with happy guests, and the couple looked splendid, Frank in his smartest uniform and Violet in the lavish dress that she had carefully made for herself. Following the ceremony, they left for a short honeymoon on the coast.

(By co-incidence they were married on the anniversary of the disastrous day that, in 1876, Major General George Armstrong Custer with the US 7th Calvary made his last stand against Crazy Horse's Sioux and Cheyenne warriors in the Battle of the Little Bighorn!)

Upon their return, the newly-weds moved in with Violet's parents at "Weybrook" for the last days of Frank's leave. Frank was delighted to learn that his younger brother Harry had, whilst he had been on holiday, arrived at Bramshott fresh from Canada. He was a member of the latest draft of reinforcements to cross the Atlantic on the SS Corsican. He was bound for the 46th battalion! It must have been a very happy reunion when they met up!

During that time Frank was introduced to Violet's friend, Flora Thompson in Liphook. He was fascinated to learn of Flora's involvement in electrical telegraphy with the Post Office. She told him that in 1900, Canadian engineer Frederick Creed had invented a system to convert morse code messages into text. Flora's role was to operate, and instruct on, the single needle machine that the Post Office now relied upon. It was because of the Grayshott branch's facility that so many customers had attended her counter to send and receive messages. More importantly he learnt that, since 1913, it was possible to send 8 morse messages through one pair of wires simultaneously. This was fascinating information for Frank as a signals officer.

The three of them got along well, and when they parted Flora felt compelled to wish her friend's husband good luck. Thinking of her dear brother she urged Frank to stay safe.

Arriving back in France on the 3rdJuly 1917, Frank slotted back into his role. He was happy to learn that his friend Betty Stevenson was now working as a YMCA driver based at nearby Étaples. He often had to attend meetings around the divisional area, usually travelling on his horse. His men were kept extremely busy laying telephone lines and transmitting confidential messages. In an atmosphere where French troops had started to mutiny, Frank soon realized that plans were being made for another big Allied push. This was to be in the region of a nearby place called Passchendaele. It was considered essential for Britain's survival to fight here to prevent the continual loss of shipping from submarines based on the Belgium coast.

In the build up to the battle, Frank was tasked to assist a Captain Routh of the Royal Flying Corps in briefing senior artillery officers at the No 16 squadron RFC airfield at nearby Bray.

No.16 Squadron Royal Flying Corps BE2s at Bray, in France in 1917

The objective was to give instruction about the latest air/ground wireless communications. There he first heard about and met the very interesting Major Eyres of the 145 (East Cheshire) battery of the British Royal Artillery. His unit was a heavy unit using 60-pounder field guns. They were attached to the Canadian 4th Division.

Cresswell EYRES as an Admiral in 1912

Interestingly, Major Cresswell John Eyres DSO had retired in 1912 after 40 years' service in the Royal Navy. He had reached the rank of Admiral but being a close friend of the King had been allowed despite his age, to re-join the military and serve again.

Frank didn't, however, neglect his entertainments officer role. One task was to publish the weekly Divisional newspaper. It was felt to be imperative, for the sake of good morale, to ensure that publications aimed at Canadian troops hit the right note. Humour was what was needed. Frank knew that his young brother Harry had a real gift for caricature since attending Manchester School of Art in his teens. On one of his regular visits to the 46th Battalion he sought out and encouraged Harry to accept the position of a divisional cartoonist.

An example of Harry Hall's drawings

(After the war ended, Harry made a living as a comic strip artist working for the Toronto Telegram, and later, during the Second World War, in Britain lampooning Hitler.)

****

Four weeks after Frank returned from his wedding leave, heavy rain began to fall in Flanders. Then more than 3,000 artillery pieces bombarded the German lines with 4.5 million shells. This turned the land into a swampy pulverised mire, exposing the thousands of rotting corpses of men who had been killed in previous battles. The Battle of Passchendaele had begun, and soon the attacking infantry was walking over no-man's-land, towards the enemy. A lot of moving literature was inspired by some very talented writers during these years.

ATTACK by Siegfreid Sassoon.

At dawn the ridge emerges massed and dun
In the wild purple of the glow'ring sun,
Smouldering through spouts of drifting smoke that shroud
The menacing scarred slope; and, one by one,
Tanks creep and topple forward to the wire.
The barrage roars and lifts. Then, clumsily bowed
With bombs and guns and shovels and battle-gear,
Men jostle and climb to meet the bristling fire.
Lines of grey, muttering faces, masked with fear,
They leave their trenches, going over the top,
While time ticks blank and busy on their wrists,
And hope, with furtive eyes and grappling fists,
Flounders in mud. O Jesus, make it stop!

****

Fourteen Victoria Crosses were awarded for heroic performances on that one day. After three weeks, 70,000 British men had been killed or wounded.

Frank's brother Harry, who was in the trenches from the start, was perhaps fortunate in that he suffered from mustard gas exposure on the 30thOctober and was taken out of the line to recover.

The Battle lasted for three and a half months, and when it ended on 14th November that year, the allies had suffered 275,000 casualties (including 15,600 Canadian soldiers). One of those men killed on 25th October 1917 was Frank's friend Harry Corrigan.

FUTILITY by Wilfred Owen

Move him into the sun—
Gently its touch woke him once,
At home, whispering of fields half-sown.
Always it woke him, even in France,
Until this morning and this snow.
If anything might rouse him now
The kind old sun will know.
Think how it wakes the seeds—
Woke once the clays of a cold star.
Are limbs, so dear-achieved, are sides
Full-nerved, still warm, too hard to stir?

> Was it for this the clay grew tall?
> —O what made fatuous sunbeams toil
> To break earth's sleep at all?

****

During this titanic battle, Frank was working from Divisional headquarters. He was never-the-less still at considerable risk from enemy action. One afternoon in late August 1917, a week after his brother had been gassed, Frank set out on a routine visit to some of his men who were laying wire near to the front line. He was riding his horse Betty on a muddy road, and he found himself gradually catching up with a British Artillery battery which was re-locating. Frank recognised the unit's mounted officer as young Lieutenant called James (Jim) Iveson, who he knew quite well, and they rode together chatting for a while. The Battery was still attached to Frank's Division and had supported it during the recent battles in the area. Frank frequently visited in a liaison role, and he enquired about his other friends, Lieutenants Davidson, and Elliot. He then asked about their very eccentric Battery commander, Major Cresswell John Eyres, who he had met earlier in the year.

The "behind the lines" roads were often targeted by the enemy

Suddenly, there were the screaming sounds of shells approaching and then close-by shattering detonations on the road ahead. The officers saw that the battery was being targeted, and Frank's companion immediately galloped off to see to his men. Frank meanwhile wheeled Betty about to escape the danger area. Before he could find cover, a devastating explosion blew him

89

from Betty's back. Frank deafened and dazed staggering amazingly uninjured to his feet. He looked across the road and saw his beloved horse, lying beside the road and badly wounded. Frank rushed over to his friend, but in her wild agony, the horse kicked him hard with her hind legs, in the back.

Getting groggily to his feet, Frank saw immediately that his dear Betty's grievous wounds were going to be fatal. He knew what he had to do and had seen many others having to do it before. Despite by now being hardened and practical, Frank had to force himself to put away any sentimental thoughts. Looking into Betty's wild eyes he drew his revolver and shot her in the head. The shellfire stopped as suddenly as it had started.

Using a discarded rifle as a prop, he hobbled the two miles back to Divisional Headquarters at Anzin on foot. He called for his batman, before having a wash and changing into clean clothes. Frank then went back to work, but later that day he began to feel really ill. He developed a constant cough, was nauseous and his back was hurting from Betty's kick. By evening his skin had turned blotchy red and was very sore. Frank was however so inundated with vital tasks that he persevered with his labour for a full seven days before being forced to seek medical help. Arriving at the Divisional medical centre he sought out Corporal 'Shaun'. Frank was immediately diagnosed as suffering from exposure to mustard gas poisoning.

(Note: Mustard gas is heavier than air and so lies beneath it and close to the ground. Consequently, shell holes could still be tainted for weeks after it was deployed. It seems that my grandfather received a comparatively mild dose of this potentially deadly poison.)

Frank was straight away sent by train to the Boulogne military hospital near the coast. There he was examined by an experienced doctor who confirmed the diagnosis. Betty Stevenson drove her Y.M.C.A. car the few miles to see Frank after she had been told that he was there. Following initial treatment, Frank was shipped back to Bramshott hospital in England for a period of recuperation. During his time in the care of the Canadian nursing staff he renewed several of the friendships that he had formed on previous visits. His new wife Violet visited him each day. Frank's medical notes of this time showed that he was likely to make a physical recovery from the gassing but that he was experiencing, amongst other symptoms, an alarming degree of phobia.

The war poet **Siegfried Sassoon's** poem illustrates the state of many soldier's minds after prolonged periods in a battle zone.

Repression of War Experience

Now light the candles; one; two; there's a moth;
What silly beggers they are to blunder in
And scorch their wings with glory, liquid flame—
No, no, not that, — it's bad to think of war,
When thoughts you've gagged all day come back to scare you;
And it's been proved that soldiers don't go mad
Unless they lose control of ugly thoughts
That drive them out to jabber among the trees.

Now light your pipe; look, what a steady hand.
Draw a deep breath; stop thinking and count fifteen,
And you're as right as rain...
Why won't it rain?...
I wish there'd be a thunderstorm to-night,
With bucketsful of water to sluice the dark,
And make the roses hang their dripping heads.

Books; what a jolly company you are,
Standing so quiet and patient on their shelves,
Dressed in dim brown, and black, and white, and green,
And every kind of colour. Which will you read?
Come on; O do read something; they're so wise.
I tell you all the wisdom of the world
Is waiting for you on those shelves; and yet
You sit and gnaw your nails, and let your pipe out,
And listen to the silence: on the ceiling
There's one big, dizzy moth that bumps and flutters;
And in the breathless air outside the house
The garden waits for something that delays.
There must be crowds of ghosts among the trees, —
Not people killed in battle, — they're in France,
But horrible shapes in shrouds — old men who died
Slow, natural deaths, — old men with ugly souls,
Who wore their bodies out with ugly sins.

You're quiet and peaceful, summering safe at home;
You'd never think there was a bloody war on! ...
O yes, you would ... why, you can hear the guns.
Hark! Thud, thud, thud, — quite soft ... they never cease —
Those whispering guns — Oh Christ, I want to go out
And screech at them to stop — I'm going crazy;
I'm going stark, staring mad because of the guns.

****

On 23rd November 1917 Frank left hospital and was granted sick leave. He spent it at "Weybrook". (It was during this leave that Violet became pregnant with their first child).

After two weeks Frank re-attended the hospital suffering from inflamed back muscles. He was treated there for five more days before being granted 16 additional days sick leave. This allowed him to spend his Christmas with Violet. At the end of December, Frank returned to his unit in Belgium to learn to his huge relief that the Battle of Passchendaele was over.

He resumed his duties at divisional headquarters, and as soon as he could find the time, he visited his brother Harry who was back with the 46th Battalion. He too had recovered from his gassing, and on the 7thFebruary

1918, he was awarded a 'Good Conduct Badge'. (An inverted chevron to be worn on the left sleeve of his tunic). Nine days after that, Harry was sent to the UK for his two weeks leave. Frank told him to make sure he visited Violet. Harry happily did so but, sadly, when he returned to his unit he was found to have been enjoying himself a little too much. He and his friends were drunk. This infringement of military law resulted in them each being sentenced to 14 days field punishment!

Soldiers found guilty of offences against military discipline were likely to be sentenced to confinement like this for two hours each day for several days as a punitive measure

It didn't however stop him continuing to draw his cartoons with which to illustrate the divisional newspaper.

Frank (having a commission) managed to get UK leave approved yet again and boarded the leave boat on 16th February 1918. Violet was delighted to have him back with her again after 6 months, especially as she was now expecting.

It was during this leave that Violet told Frank all about her exciting new customer Mabel Dolmetsch. Mabel, with her husband Arnold and their children, had moved to Haslemere. The Dolmetsch's were world-renowned musicians and makers of replica period musical instruments. Their friends included the writers George Bernard Shaw and W.B. Yeats.

This French family had left Paris in 1914, to get away from the anticipated German invasion. They settled in Hampstead, London but eventually felt it necessary, because of the Zeppelin's attacks on that city, to escape to the countryside.

(Despite 77 airships being shot down over England, they managed to kill 700 civilians with their bombing)

The Dolmetsch family performing their music

After leaving London, the Dolmetsch's had spent a few months living in a friend's rented cottage at Thursley village. Happy there, they spent their time looking for a house to buy in nearby Haslemere. Whilst living in the cottage they had befriended a French-Canadian army unit based at the adjacent Witley Camp. There they had been happy to perform a series of concerts for the soldier's entertainment.

After a few months, the Dolmetsch's found and bought a house called 'Jesses' on the outskirts of Haslemere. Their move coincided with Christmas 1917 when it was bitterly cold and snowing. A local farmer had been contracted to move their belongings, but his horses couldn't get up the slippery hill. Remembering his Canadian army friends, Mr Dolmetsch contacted a Major Coulder and asked him for his soldiers' help. As a result, the house contents were promptly and successfully moved by horse-drawn Canadian Army waggons.

After the move, the Dolmetsch's opened a workshop at 'Jesses' to make their musical instruments (owning one of which, became a status symbol in smart society).

Mabel and her husband travelled widely to perform at concerts, and later in life she appeared on the front cover of Vogue magazine, wearing clothes made for her by Violet.

Their children Rudolph, Carl, Cecile and Nathalie also became very accomplished musicians. Mabel herself was a performer of ancient dances, as well as being a gifted musician.

(Later in her life, Mabel often gave free Dolmetsch public concerts tickets to her dressmaker. These performances were held in Haslemere, and Violet often took her young daughter Beatrice (Betty) with her as members of the audience. Betty consequently became a lifelong enthusiast for classical music. When she had a family of her own, she transferred this love of melody to her sons. Tony and Mark Walton in turn developed into being acclaimed musicians in the antipodes).

Sadly, Mabel's son Rudolph was killed in December 1942. He was a wartime Royal Artillery bandmaster on the White Star line 'SS Ceramic' on route to Australia. The ship was being used as a troopship when she was sunk by a German U-boat in the Atlantic. 656 people died, including the bandmaster and 30 nurses. There was just one survivor).

At the end of his leave, Frank caught the Army ferry back to France and to his job at headquarters. Having once again experienced the sharp painful contrast between the barbaric battlefield violence and the harmonious haven of Violet's Haslemere, his senses were reeling. He could not name his new horse with the name of the one that he had shot. He refused to allow too close an affection for her to develop in his heart.

A few weeks later, on 30th April 1918, Frank was overjoyed to meet up with his youngest brother Gerald. He arrived amongst the latest draft of reinforcements into the 46th battalion.

They and brother Harry talked long into the night over Frank's bottle of Johnny Walker. Frank and Harry wanted news of the family in Canada and the States. Harry and Gerald wanted to know all about their new sister-in-law Violet. Frank answered all their questions and explained that she had agreed to move with him to Canada as soon as the war was over.

In early June 1918, Frank was shocked to learn that his friend Betty Stevenson had been killed. She had died in an air raid whilst typically driving other Y.M.C.A. workers to safety.

Her job was supposed to have been safe and well away from danger. Frank was devastated and yet once again had to stifle and bury his deep sorrow. He cried when on his own.

Somewhere in France.
Betty and Archie.

Betty with her lorry

Betty on her last
home leave

It is a fact that most soldiers join as privates and finish their military careers in the same rank.

Leaders however must be found, and so senior ranks are constantly on the look-out for people to promote, who other soldiers will follow without reluctance. Occasionally someone stands out as a natural leader, who others instinctively respect and who has the ability to take those others with him.

On 1st June 1918, Frank learned with delight that his young brother Gerald was awarded a 'Good Conduct Badge'. Having displayed fine leadership qualities in his short time with the 46th Battalion, this 25-year-old Private, was identified as being suitable for promotion, jumping three ranks, straight to that of Staff Sergeant. (This rapid advancement is an indication of the desiccating effect of the high casualty rate of platoon leaders experienced by the 46th Battalion on the front line).

Since February an influenza epidemic had been developing into a pandemic. Many soldiers in Europe had been badly affected during the first wave of what was then referred to as "the Spanish Flue" or just "the flue". The Army authorities were anxious that the disease's effects did not cause a lowering of morale amongst the troops. Consequently, there was a media blackout imposed and the increasing spread and effects of the terrible ailment was not widely known.

Young people aged between 20 and 30 were particularly vulnerable to the virus. It affected men more severely than it did women, although it did cause many abortions. A second wave, much more deadly than the first, started in late August 1918.

The fighting continued to put all three Hall brothers at enormous daily risk, but as November approached the killing was drawing towards a juddering and then sudden cessation.

Back in Surrey on 5th September 1918, Violet was at Guildford Hospital giving birth to her first child, Beatrice (Betty) Evelyn. As soon as Frank got the news of his daughter's arrival, he applied for a UK furlough.

On 26th October 1918 he was granted 14 days leave, which he of course spent at Haslemere. The moment he got home Violet presented him with seven-week-old Betty for the first time. As he cradled this new life in his arms, Frank found himself sobbing uncontrollably. He couldn't explain why to Violet, as he doubted that she would understand his supressed emotions. That night he lay awake until dawn. He spent his leave enraptured by his new daughter.

Two days after his return to France, the Armistice was declared.

As a Divisional Signals Officer, he was one of the first soldiers in the Canadian 4th Division to hear that the fighting was over for good. An eery silence settled over the blood-soaked battlefields. It was Fank's duty to pass this incredulous news onto the sceptical troops. However, he was not yet allowed to tell them of the Spanish Flue which was raging worldwide and was eventually to kill over 50 million people.

During their 27 months of combat on the Western Front prior to the Armistice, the 46th Battalion lost 1,443 men killed and 3,484 men wounded (a 91.5% casualty rate).

They fought in sixteen battles and were nicknamed "The Suicide Battalion". As a fighting force it was highly respected, and the men maintained their magnificent morale throughout.

The 46th Battalion Canadian Expeditionary Force cap badge

In early December, Frank was again granted two weeks UK leave. His brother, newly promoted Staff Sergeant Gerald Hall, was also given two weeks off and was able to spend Christmas Day with Frank, Violet, and little Betty. It was a brief visit for Gerald, as on the 28thDecember he had to return to his unit in France.

(Sadly, when he arrived back with the battalion, he had misplaced his issued holdall and contents. For this he was disciplined by the Military authorities).

Now that the fighting over, the Canadian government's stated aim was to return all Canadian soldiers to their homes in Canada as soon as possible.

Shortly after Christmas 1918, whilst he was still with Violet in Haslemere, Frank received an army posting order. With immediate effect, he was transferred onto the administration strength at Bramshott Camp as part of the Repatriation Team. Frank was to work again with Colonel Herbert Snell.

****

Chapter 9

"Canada, so far from my Home"

After Christmas 1918, Frank started work for Colonel Snell at Bramshott Camp. Haslemere was within easy cycling distance and so, as a newly married officer, he was able to obtain permission to live away from camp.

With little delay he moved in with Violet at her parents' house. Thus, the courtship was over and these two young people began the journey of learning how to be a conventional married couple, and how to be parents to three-month-old Betty.

By 1919 Frank's wife was an attractive 25-year-old mother and was successful in her home-based dressmaking career. She was capable and strongminded, with a circle of friends and with wealthy customers in the area. Her Mother, Emma, helped to look after the baby.

Life in a war zone changes you

Quite differently, Frank was a seasoned veteran of the bloodiest war in world history. During two years in or near the frontline, he had frequently been in mortal danger and had become accustomed to an uncomfortable, spartan life. He had been stretched, and successfully held important, demanding roles at the cutting edge of technology. As he developed, Frank had found it necessary to become very decisive, and very self-sufficient. He had learned not to dwell upon reflections about the past.

He had followed, and when necessary enforced, a rigid discipline in an environment where any show of emotional upset was seen as weakness. Many of his pals from Moose Jaw had been killed in the most violent of ways. More of them had been injured and some were horribly disfigured. He knew men who had lost their minds or disgraced themselves. Quite frequently a soldier's acts of extreme heroism were considered by their mates to be quite unexceptional in the circumstances. He had little time for trivialities and frivolity.

Frank was to be mentioned in Despatches for carrying on with his essential job for several days, after being subjected to mustard gas poisoning. The lasting symptoms from this injury included phobia and sleeplessness. He also suffered from skin and respiratory damage.

This daily dangerous grind had forced Frank to develop a hard, unsympathetic nature, along with a dark sense of humour. He and his comrades had acquired a linguistic wall of slang unfathomable to others. They cultivated an extreme pride in the accomplishments of the Canadian Army, combined with deep senses of patriotism and comradeship.

He had not been rewarded with any promotion beyond the rank of that which he had when he arrived from Canada. This neglect had added a despondent element to his character.

Military combatants are expected to kill the enemy, sometimes at close quarters. Soldiers in a battle zone must operate in extreme conditions. The troops may be traumatised under constant shellfire for days or even weeks on end, with little hot nourishment. They will experience extreme tiredness, unsanitary conditions, and abject fear.

It is contrary to the nature of most men to live like this, and so during wartime the authorities must motivate and condition men to act abnormally.

Loyalty, confidence, patriotism, and an encouraged hatred of the enemy can all play a part. However strong drink has been used for centuries to induce "Dutch Courage" into men about to go into battle. Its effects boosted morale, reduced fear and acted as a combat motivator. As a coping mechanism it dulled and controlled the nerves. It calmed soldiers down after battle and warmed their cold wet bodies in icy conditions. Rum allowed them sleep at night. There was more to winning than patriotism and fighting spirit. However, the long-term bad effects of using alcohol to excess are well known.

During World War One the Temperance Movements of both Britain and Canada, were very active in doing all that they could to stop the consumption of alcohol in society generally. Nevertheless, following a Royal Navy tradition started centuries before, the Army authorities provided a rum ration to all troops.

Waggon loads of it were delivered regularly from the provisions stores to unit's Quartermasters. It arrived in gallon jars marked S.R.D. (Special

Rum Demerara). It was an extremely strong 86% proof, dark tarry spirit that made a man's eyes water if taken neat. A tot of 70ml (2.5 fluid ounces) was issued twice weekly for all troops not on the front line. Those in the trenches were given a tot every day, distributed under the supervision of junior officers. An additional double tot was authorised for those going over the top or carrying out a particularly hazardous mission.

__Soldiers became dependant upon the rum ration, delivered daily, in these jars__

__Apart from anything else it help them to sleep when they needed to__

Often it was mixed with sweetened tea, coffee, or cocoa because it massively improved the chemical taste of water that was delivered in petrol drums. Yet another double tot was waiting for the men to drink on their return from action. Due to the inevitable casualties, there was always a lot of rum left over after a battle.

The rum issue could be withdrawn as a punishment used to enforce discipline. Effective officers regularly used it as a motivational tool, and as a reward. (e.g. Soldiers recovering mutilated rotting bodies from no man's land under fire, would receive an extra ration. "To take the taste of dead men out of my mouth"). When soldiers were in "rest" behind the lines, or on leave, drunkenness was part of their toolkit, used to forget temporarily their more troubling experiences. Estaminets (cafes) were established by local people, providing a cabaret, selling food, prostitutes' services and, of course, drink (mainly beer, and wine).

After WW1 the Black Watch Battalion's very experienced medical officer giving evidence at an enquiry on the subject of shell shock stated, "Had it not been for the effects of the rum ration, I do not think we should have won the war". Rum was even administered as a treatment for exhaustion, hypothermia, flue and wounds.

The casualty attrition rate and consequential stress experienced by young officers was extremely high. In addition to the rum, they were permitted access to whisky and other spirits (e.g., French brandy). As a result, many of them became fully fledged alcoholics.

__An extra tot was often issued as a reward__

Like most of his fellow officers, Frank drank a lot. He had five times experienced the sharp confusing contrast between the battle zone and peaceful Surrey.

Quite different rules of behaviour applied in each environment. These marked divergences in values had calloused his emotions and permanently warped his personality. He was not the same man as he had been when he and Violet had first met and danced together in 1916.

Frank's new job was an important one involving reconciling conflicting interests. The Armistice of 11th November 1918 was a truce, not the end of the war. It was a lull so that the warring sides could negotiate the terms of peace. In effect, the war didn't end until 1919. If the Allies demobilised too many of their troops, that would affect their credibility in peace negotiations. It would be seen as reducing their ability to resume the fight and so lessen the pressure on the German authorities to make concessions. Therefore, sufficient troops had to be kept available as a credible threat in the event of German non-compliance. Choices as to who to send home first caused uncertainty and dissatisfaction. The Canadian Government wanted fit men and married men home first to aid their economy. They also wanted men who were casualties to be treated before returning to Canada. The soldiers were infuriated that some men who had never been near to the front line should go home before those who had actually fought for the Empire.

The ordinary Canucks (Canadian troops) thinking that the war was over wanted no delay in their return home. Expediency was delayed by post-war British industrial unrest and a shortage of troop ships. Pre-repatriation medical boards had a big effect upon the men's discharge pensions at home. To vent their frustration, some of the Canadian troops indulged in a surge of disorder and ill-discipline hoping to force the issue.

Due to his experiences in France, Frank was suffering from his own demons at the time. He knew that if he were classified as being ill, his own return could be delayed. So, like a lot of men in a similar position, he did his best to hide his problems. This must have been difficult in the pressurised job that he was doing. Bramshott camp was packed with thousands of men who all wanted to go home.

Red Cross nurses in France

__The nurses earned huge respect from the men__

From September 1918, the Spanish Flu epidemic spread to the UK. It was to kill millions of people worldwide. The disease mainly attacked young men and often killed victims within days. Despite dedicated nursing care, the Canadian Military Hospital at Bramshott lost 776 soldier patients to the pandemic, most of whom were recovering battle casualties. They are buried in churchyards in and around Bramshott.

__Canadian military graves in Bramshott churchyard__

On 28th April 1919 the 46th Battalion, with brothers Harry and Gerald, were deloused and shipped from Le Havre back to Bramshott Camp. There they were delighted to meet Frank and their old commanding officer, Herbert Snell. With some help, the Battalion was fast-tracked through. Gerald met up with Frank and Violet as often as they could.

Several of the men in the battalion joined in the rush of thousands of Canucks to tie the knot with local girls. They took advantage of the reduced cost, fast-tracked ceremonies that had been introduced, to marry their English sweethearts before they left for Canada.

During this frantic period, on 3rd May part of the Battalion travelled up to London to take part in the end of the war Victory Parade for Dominion Troops. After returning to Bramshott Camp there were a few false starts before they finally sailed for Canada on the 28th of May. After crossing back over the Atlantic, the 46th Battalion disembarked at Quebec and were demobilised in Moose Jaw on the 9th of June 1919. Three months later, Frank was still working in repatriation management, but had been relocated to nearby Witley Camp. Witley was classed as a "Concentration Camp" and was crowded to capacity with more Canadians anxious to go home. The pressure of work on Frank must have been enormous, and one can only guess at the domestic friction that it caused at 34 Kings Road. Violet saw that Frank was more serious than he had been, and that he now drank too much. She sympathised when he woke in the middle of the night, sweating and coughing and shouting. She was hurt when he showed so little sympathy for her problems, and that he had developed a short temper. However, she recognised the difficult time that he had been through and believed that with patience and love he would recover to be the Frank that he had been.

Violet was anxious about when and how all three of them were going to travel to Canada. She was now wondering what she had got herself into by marrying this Canadian soldier. She was apprehensive about leaving the close familiarity of her home, friends, business, parents, and wider family. She feared to travel to an unknown future so far away.

After much discreet enquiry, Frank managed to get an appointment at far-away Buxton Military Hospital. This Canadian Medical Centre specialised in the treatment of soldiers who were suffering from various forms of war-sustained nervous exhaustion.

He returned to Violet after a week of treatment. Soon after that he received word that he and his new family were to travel to Glasgow by rail and sail together to Montreal in Quebec on the troopship SS Corsican. (Note: The same ship that brother Harry had travelled from Canada on). Frank handed Violet a booklet issued by the Canadian Government Repatriation Committee. The introduction assured a "sincere and friendly welcome to future homemakers in Canada". It contained details of the impending journey, advice about clothing, and suggestions as to what food and milk formula to buy for her baby. They were to travel with returning soldiers, and with some other wives and their dependants. (Some of them were Canadian wives who had travelled to England from Canada, to be near to their Army husbands).

The extended Furlonger family's contacts proved very useful in arranging for Violet's luggage to be shipped from Haslemere to Moose Jaw. She made sure that her Singer sewing machine was carefully packaged for the journey.

On the appointed morning, Violet and Betty were helped onto her father's best cart and taken by her parents the short distance to Haslemere railway station. Her luggage was taken there in a separate Funnel and Furlonger's waggon. There was a small crowd of well-wishers on the platform to see them off.

One can easily imagine her parent's emotions at wishing goodbye to their beloved only daughter and grandchild. Violet was popular and well thought of locally, and the well-wishers must have included dear friends who never expected to see her again.

Amidst the many tears and fond farewells, the Liphook train puffed and clanked into the station. Frank had reserved seats in a compartment in the first-class carriage for them to travel in. The train was virtually empty, and a pre-briefed soldier quickly showed them to their carriage. All too soon doors were slammed shut, and a shrieked whistle proceeded a jerk as the train pulled away from the platform. Last endearments were shouted, kisses blown, and they were off.

No sooner had the engine driver reached a cruising speed than he applied the brakes to slow down. Ten minutes after leaving Haslemere, the train was pulling up at the small station serving Witley town.

There a very different sight met Violet. The platform was packed with Khaki uniforms. Hundreds of happy Canuks from Witley Camp, were on their way home. The officer in charge of the draft, was a grinning Lieutenant Frank Hall, who waved happily to Violet as the train squealed to a halt. After loading baggage and men the train was off again.

Frank held his baby daughter and watched contemplatively, as his young wife waved goodbye from the open window. Once the train was under way, he introduced Violet to three young women who were to share their six-seat compartment. They were each dressed as military nurses and were from Bramshott hospital. Their rank was equivalent to that of a male Lieutenant, and they shared the same privileges. Frank had got to know these three nurses from his time as a patient in the hospital. They had all co-operated with Frank's proposal of marriage and been guests at the marriage ceremony. They too were returning home for discharge in Saskatchewan. Having these women travel with her during the journey was a huge relief to Violet. As Frank left to return to his men, he was satisfied to see them all chatting happily together.

An hour later the passengers alighted into the thronging crowds on Waterloo Station platform. Although Frank's duty was to his troops, he had adequately instructed his Sergeants to take charge of the men. In that way he was free to help Violet with Betty and the luggage. It must have been very stressful for Violet, who had never travelled far from rural Haslemere. In London the heaving noisy crowds of people and the perplexing atmosphere of smelly smog added to the strangeness for Frank's wife. It caused the baby to cry unconsolably.

Many soldiers waited impatiently to be demobilised

Eventually the party reached a convoy of Army trucks and charabancs parked by the roadside outside the station. A confusing thirty minutes followed whilst Frank assured himself that all his men were present and briefed. Then they boarded the transports for the short journey to nearby Euston station. Met by guides and following prominent signs, they all soon alighted onto the train that was to travel over half the length of Britain to Glasgow in Scotland.

Violet again had seats in the First-Class carriage. The carriage was linked to the restaurant and it was divided into six apartments, joined by a narrow corridor on the left which led to a spacious bathroom. She again shared the apartment with her new friends, the three nurses.

At 11 a.m. the train began its long journey. Soon Violet settled with a sigh into her seat and began to feed her fretful baby hoping to then lull her to sleep. Sighing with relief, she realised how tired and hungry she was herself. Without further ado she ordered a particularly good lunch from the waiter. As she ate, she gazed out of the window at the countryside flashing past and thought of her parents and of home. Violet wondered how much she would miss familiar England when she arrived in the strange land on the other side of the Atlantic. While thinking she drifted into a restless sleep.

Violet slept on until, with an abrupt jerk, the train stopped to top up the boilers and take on coal at the Crewe sidings. The baby began to cry again.

Freed from his duties for a while, Frank joined them all, and he and Violet talked about their future. Violet noticed with slight unease that he had been drinking again.

After passing through Preston, Lancaster, Penrith, and Carlisle they crossed the Scottish border at Gretna Green and continued north to Motherwell and then into Glasgow Central station. After an 8-hour journey from London they were all weary beyond belief. It was a dark and rainy night, and the furthest that Violet had ever been from home. She was not able to understand what on earth the local Glaswegians were saying, so unfamiliar with their accent was she!

There was to be no rest. Parked in a line outside the station was a convoy of horse drawn vehicles. The travellers had yet to reach the River Clyde dockyards, some 6 miles away. Frank had to keep a close eye on his large party of men, some of whom were by now hopelessly drunk. He was not able to help Violet very much, and it was fortunate that she had the nurse's help to successfully manage her baby and luggage.

Finally, at 9 pm, they all set off. Squashed up on a bench seat, she hummed softly to baby Betty and noticed passing through the small towns of Govan and Kingston. Before long they arrived at the impressive entrance to George V docks on the south bank of the Clyde River. Their transport convoy continued a short distance, and then came to a halt on the dockside. Towering over them was the huge black hull of a transatlantic liner.

__They were beside the SS Corsican__

Frank was too occupied to help his wife but had arranged for his trusted Sergeant and three men to help her, the baby, and the nurses to their cabins. Thus, all the luggage was carried up the gangplank to the ladies' shipboard accommodation. Violet was happy to see that her new friends shared the cabin next to hers. She had never been on a ship before and felt daunted by this new experience. The stewards were helpful and told her that the ship was sailing the next morning and would dock at Montreal in the evening 5 days hence.

Violet saw to the baby and had herself a late but welcome dinner in her cabin. By 11 p.m. she could not keep her eyes open any longer and went to bed. She was woken after midnight by an equally exhausted Frank. He knocked on the cabin door and was soon asleep beside her.

Tossing and turning, Violet was prevented from sleeping by ruminations drifting through her head. She was impressed at the obvious deference that Frank was given by the men, most of whom he had never commanded in France. He didn't raise his voice, and when he appeared they all became quiet and look towards him expectantly. Whenever he gave a quiet instruction, it was acknowledged with a very natural "Yes Sir". She remembered that most of these men would shortly be civilians again. The obvious respect that they had for her young husband was something that she struggled to understand, as it was quite outside her experience.

Seven hours after midnight, they were disturbed by the rumble of engines and the clanging of bells. Looking out of their porthole Violet saw that the ship was moving away from the dock. It was the 12thSeptember 1919.

After breakfast Frank took his spouse up on deck to show her the Clydebank unfolding, as the ship, packed with 2,000 passengers negotiated its way towards the Firth of Clyde. She could feel the drumming of the mighty engines even at slow speed. Soon they were free from the land and steaming faster towards the open sea. Violet faced away from the cool breeze and gazed towards the ship's stern with trepidation. The receding view reminded her again of the finality of leaving her homeland. She leant against the ship's rail and quietly wept.

Early on that first day, she was advised by the nurses that cases of the Spanish Flu had been found amongst the soldiers. She was advised to keep a distance from other people and wear a facemask when other men or women were in the same room. Violet took their advice seriously because she knew some people in Haslemere who had contracted the disease. Using a petticoat hem, she made up some masks for herself, Frank, and the baby to use.

The ship's speed increased as it headed up the North Channel and approached the Mull of Kintyre, glimpsed on the starboard side.

That evening Violet saw the last hazy sighting of land as the ship rounded to the north of Ireland where the Malin Head lighthouse flashes could be seen. The ship altered course slightly to port and then they were truly in the Atlantic Ocean.

Fortunately, neither Violet nor Betty were affected by sea sickness.

Their ship steamed out of the Firth of Clyde,
leaving Violet's home behind

The last sign of land that they saw was the lighthouse signal from Tory Island. The three nurses were able to remember these names from their outward passage.

During the crossing and Violet soon got into the seaboard routine. Frank was able to spend most of each day with Violet. They talked about their future plans, read books to each other, played cards and Violet asked in detail about the family members she would meet in Moose Jaw. The time passed quickly.

On the evening of the 17th of September, the Corsican left the Atlantic and entered the Cabot Straight, and on into the Gulf of St. Lawrence. At first the passengers couldn't see the land on either side of the ship. However, as they moved up the St Lawrence River, they were able to make out the lights of small settlements on both shores. Violet held Frank's hand and looked deep into his eyes for reassurance. They watched with wonder as the ship cruised slowly under the almost completed, longest cantilever bridge in the world.

__Quebec Bridge (at that time, still under construction)__

The passengers were advised that they were to prepare for disembarkation the next morning, right after breakfast. It was ten in the evening before their ship reached and then steamed past Quebec City. Violet and Frank were so tired that they went to bed. Seven hours later they were roused by a maritime steam whistle, which screeched a greeting as the ship approached the Port of Montreal. Looking out of a porthole Violet gazed in wonder and saw that they had arrived at a huge city. The voyage was complete, five and a half days after leaving Glasgow. Frank apologised as he left to attend to more of his military responsibilities.

The port authorities were accustomed to mass immigration and their methods were smooth and practiced. As the passengers left the gangplanks, they were directed to a nearby processing building. Their luggage was taken by porters to an adjacent warehouse. The processing was to ensure that the passengers were not ill and had the right authority to enter Canada. This was especially important due to the worldwide pandemic.

As an officer's wife Violet's procedures were carried out more quickly and politely than was the case for the less fortunate steerage class passengers. She and Betty were soon on the way by taxi to the nearby Canadian Pacific Railway Station. As she entered the great hall, she was greeted with sights that were unfamiliar to her, and by the exciting smells of burning wood and the sounds of hot steam. She was aghast as she looked up at the colossal locomotive and carriages which were poised beside the platform. They seemed twice the size of the ordinary engines that regularly puffed past her house in, oh so far away, Haslemere. Violet and her baby were directed into a family carriage, and her luggage was put in by the helpful porters.

__Returning Canadians board a train at Montreal in 1919__

She was delighted to find she was again sharing her self-contained 'immigrant' compartment with her friends, the three nurses. They were to travel to their own homes in Regina for most of Violet's journey. Soon an agent came around the carriages taking food orders. Violet had been warned to expect this and knew that she would be cooking her own food during the next few days.

Once the train was loaded with the soldiers, it set off on its long journey, and onto the next stage of Violet's adventure.

****

Chapter 10.

Moose Jaw 1919

The mood of the three nurses was subdued at the start of the rail journey, having worked long hours in the medical wards whilst on board the ship. When Violet asked if everything was alright, they described spending their voyage duty time nursing soldiers and other passengers who had become ill after contracting the dreadful Spanish Flu. Despite receiving intensive care, several of the patients had died and had been buried at sea. The nurses were depressed at watching happy healthy people go downhill so quickly. Those infected passengers who had arrived alive in Canada had been quarantined by the immigration authorities at Montreal, for fear that they would further spread the disease into Canada. Fortunately, Frank and Violet did not catch the virus.

(Despite all precautions, a significant number of soldiers who survived the war died of Spanish Flu before, during or after their return to Canada. Thousands of family members who flocked to welcome their soldiers home, were infected by the close contact of greeting them back. This contamination, and cross-contamination had added to the 60,000 Canadian fatalities in battle. Many children were orphaned, and umpteen families were left with no primary wage earner).

After leaving Montreal City the train branched away from the St. Lawrence River and for three hours rattled along in a westerly direction. Violet and Frank were enchanted by the beautiful Quebec countryside arrayed before them that September morning. After crossing the Prince of Wales bridge into Ontario, the locomotive slowed down as it approached the central railway station at a city which they saw was named Ottawa. A former lumber town on the south bank of a mighty river, it was now the capital city of the whole of Canada. Violet examined the platform hawker's food and couldn't resist buying some extra. Fresh French baguettes, and other irresistibly French type snack food, added to her little store.

With no delay, the engine's thirsty boiler was filled with water and its ravenous bunker topped up with wood. After a small exchange of passengers at the long platform, the guard shouted his warnings, and a loud whistle blew. The locomotive erupted clouds of noisy steam, jerked and they were off again, heading ever westwards. Through the windows the passengers saw that they streaked through places with familiar names, such as Renfrew and Pembroke. They strained to see but caught only the briefest display and then it was gone. A glimpsed name board, a face, a horse cart impressed on the mind. The seemingly endless miles caused them to lose all track of time. Violet was just beginning to realise how vast Canada really was.

Two hours after thundering through the small town of North Bay, they felt their train begin to decelerate. Eventually after dinner it pulled up at Sudbury station. Described as a city, it was no bigger than Violet's hometown. Sudbury was originally settled by immigrants as a lumber town. It has an amazing 330 lakes within its boundaries and is surrounded by mountains. The later discovery of nickel and copper had made it an important mining centre. However, the resultant acid rain added to the denuding of tree cover had caused a bare unattractive landscape. Violet was glad that, soon after refuelling, the locomotive pulled away from the platform to start a long night journey, ever westwards, towards Thunder Bay.

Passing small settlements and towns on the north shore of a mighty lake, they thundered on. They steamed past, in tempting succession, Ramsey, Dalton, White River, Rossport and Red Rock. If they stopped to refuel, it was whilst the new Mrs Hall was asleep. After three days and nights they pulled up at a long platform on the northwest edge of Lake Superior.

Peering with weary eyes through the window into the uncertain light of that warm September evening, Violet and Frank saw that they were at Fort William, part of Thunder Bay in Ontario. They were more than halfway through their rail journey.

Whilst Frank saw to his military duties, metallic clangs, slammed doors, and hoarse shouting made sleep for Violet impossible. She soothed her infant by singing her soft lullabies. During the next 13 hours the train covered 500 miles of track, entering Manitoba Province before reaching the city of Winnipeg. The Atlantic was 1,800 miles behind them, and they were 4,000 miles from their start point. They had reached the edge of the great prairies.

Frank supervised and then bade farewell to some of his party who were leaving the train. His wife prepared another meal and some formula for the baby.

Violet had just 9 hours left of her odyssey to experience before begin-ning the next stage of her emigration adventure. Leaving Winnipeg, the train accelerated rapidly and seemed to fly across the vast almost featureless landscape. As it rattled and rocked along the track, smoke streamed back from its stack. The pungent aroma of burnt wood was something that added excitement to the passengers' experience. Frank's wife never imagined that there was such a flat place, with no hills and few trees. So very different from her home in Surrey. So very different from what she had imagined when Frank had asked her, "Come and live in Canada with me".

That night, after travelling all day, they pulled up at Regina, the capitol city of Saskatchewan. It had a very British appearance, quite unlike what they had seen in Quebec Province. (Regina is Latin for "Queen" and was so named in 1882 in honour of Queen Victoria). The three nurses left the train there.

116

Lots of promises were made, wishes of good luck and hugs and kisses. Violet felt lonely without their familiar friendly faces and would miss them terribly. The Regina soldiers were met with an impressive happy welcome from their townsfolk. As soon as the engine was refuelled, the train was off again on the final leg of Violet's journey. There was 50 miles to go.

Violet began to gather and pack her belongings. Frank left her to give briefings to the men, most of whom were leaving the train with him at Moose Jaw. He also spoke with the non-commissioned officers who were to be responsible for those remaining soldiers who would continue to their homes in Medicine Hat.

Ninety minutes later, the packed train slowed down as it approached the destination that Violet and Frank had talked about for so long. Her heart raced and she bit her lip to control her feeling of panic. They would soon be at the small prairie town of Moose Jaw. Violet could see, hear, and feel the soldiers' excitement as the platform came into sight for the straining figures at the carriage windows. They were home. It was the 23rd September 1919.

Even before the train stopped, or the doors were opened, the sounds of the welcoming band could be plainly heard. The platform was packed with family members and townsfolk eager to catch sight of their heroes returned from the war. Frank leaned through the opened window and yelled as he caught sight of his two, widely grinning, brothers, Gerald, and Harry. Waving widely, they pushed through the throng and reached Frank's carriage door just as the train stopped. Frank leapt off the coach and was immediately given the most enthusiastic of welcomes home. They were all overjoyed that by some miracle each one of them had survived their war experiences seemingly unscathed. The three men suddenly remembered, and full of apologies they handed Violet and Betty down onto the platform. The luggage followed, and then Frank pleading extenuating circumstances, rushed off to keep control of his happy disembarking troops. As instructed during his briefings, the men were soon lined up in formation, on the road outside the CPR station. A work party of militia men took charge of all their luggage and carried it in waggons to the Armoury for safekeeping.

Violet's two brothers-in-law could not hide their delight as they took charge of her. She held Betty tight as she was taken through the thronging excited crowds, off the platform, onto the road behind the station. Violet paused to watch as this latest batch of returning soldiers were marched from the station, behind the band, into the town centre. Harry explained to her that there was to be a civic reception. Delighted, cheering crowds lined the streets. Wives held up their children, and the soldiers marched with an outrageous swagger!

Soon Violet and Betty, with suitcases, bags and other paraphernalia, were put aboard a hired horse-drawn surrey.

Harry took the reins, whilst Gerald walked ahead to clear the multitude as they set off. The brothers explained what they had been doing since she had last seen them in England. Gerald told her that they were both back working as mail clerks for the railway company. All too soon the entourage arrived outside a large two-storey, wooden house. After the long journey from her parent's house, Violet had finally reached 112 Larch Road, Moose Jaw.

As the horse pulled up, four young women ran from the house porch, all talking joyously at once. They helped their sister-in-law into the parlour. There they hugged and kissed and introduced amidst much laughter and goodwill.

The house had been Frank's parents' family home before they had left Moose Jaw. William and Annie had ordered the wooden house, in kit form, through the Canadian Aladdin Co. Ltd. mail order catalogue when they had first arrived in Canada. In 1915, when Colonel Snell had closed his business and gone off to war, Frank's parents had gone to live in the city of Superior in the USA so that William could find work.

During the rest of the day and evening Frank was with his army friends, celebrating their return from the war. Violet spent the time getting to know the Hall family and she was presented with a perambulator they had bought for her. As they talked, she learnt that Evelyn was the baby of the family at just 20 years old. Dorothy was single and 23-years-old. She was however engaged and looking forward to her wedding to local man, Gordon McAdam. These two sisters worked as telephone clerks. Both of them at this time still lived in the house.

Their elder sibling Gladys was 27 years old and married to a local man. She and her husband Wellington McNabb, lived at nearby 1108 Beech Avenue. She had yet to have children and still worked as a clerk with Dorothy and Evelyn. Her brother, returned soldier Gerald, was now their lodger. The eldest of the four was Edith. She was 29 years old and lived in a tiny village called Conquest, 150 miles to the northwest of Moose Jaw. Her husband, Fred Wray, worked there on a grain farm. Edith had travelled down by train the day before Violet's arrival to be part of the family welcoming committee. Brother Harry, she was told, lodged nearby with a Moose Jaw friend at number 1258, 3rd Avenue.

During their talks, Violet was relieved to have it confirmed that she and her husband were to share the house until they found a place of their own. She went to her allotted room exhausted, but happily relieved that she had made friends with the Hall family.

Frank arrived at the house late that night, after his wife had gone to bed. He had been drinking heavily and fell asleep the moment his head hit the pillow.

****

Chapter 11

A very different life

In September 1919, when this girl from Haslemere reached Moose Jaw, it was a booming town with a population of 18,000. The province was settled mostly by pioneering British stock, with hard-working minorities from Ukraine, Germany, China, Scandinavia and the United States. Its predominant industries were grain and logging. During the war years the flat grasslands had enjoyed an economic boom. However, falling prices had caused a sharp recession and many thousands of ex-soldiers found it hard to secure employment.

Soon after arriving back from the war, Frank, in common with most of his comrades, was discharged from the Army. These hard-drinking ex-soldiers were dismayed to learn that the sale and consumption of all alcoholic drink was now against the law. This meant that it was harder to get, the cost made a hole in their family budgets, and the booze had to be drunk "on the sly".

Frank may have had an important job during the war, but like many others before and after him he found that his honed, practiced skills were not much valued in civilian life.

Vera Brittain's poem, illustrates the situation that returning soldiers faced:

The Lament of the Demobilized

'Four years,' some say consolingly. 'Oh well,
What's that? You're young. And then it must have been
A very fine experience for you!'
And they forget
How others stayed behind and just got on—
Got on the better since we were away.
And we came home and found
They had achieved, and men revered their names,
But never mentioned ours;
And no one talked heroics now, and we
Must just go back and start again once more.
'You threw four years into the melting-pot —

Did you indeed!' these others cry. 'Oh well,
The more fool you!'
And we're beginning to agree with them.

****

Frank's only non-military work experiences had been in his father's shop and later as a railway clerk. In addition, Frank's breathing was affected by the mustard gas poisoning he had suffered, and his mind was injured by his war experiences. After a few weeks of attending fruitless job interviews, he met up with his brothers and explained to them that his Army gratuity would be soon used up if he didn't find work.

Harry and Gerald had arrived home four months prior to Frank and so were ahead of him in the job queue. They had been hired as clerks by the railway company, sorting the mail on board the trains as they travelled across the country. Harold was a supervisor and told Frank that he would put in a good word for him at work. In this way ex-Private Harry used his influence to secure employment for his brother, ex-Lieutenant Frank. This must have been a little galling for the older brother, who had been used to the respect, responsibilities, and privileges of his former rank. One of the downsides of being a mail clerk was that he had to be away from home for several days at a time.

The follow-up treatment he and most others received for the damage they had suffered in the war, was virtually non-existent. They had mainly to rely on themselves, their mates, their wife's understanding care, and drink.

Searchlight

by F.S. Flint was written to record just one of the problems faced by the traumatised returned soldiers:

> **There has been no sound of guns,**
> **No roar of exploding bombs;**
> **But the darkness has an edge**
> **That grits the nerves of the sleeper.**
> **He awakens;**
> **Nothing disturbs the stillness,**
> **Save perhaps the light, slow flap,**
> **Once only of the curtain**
> **Dim in the darkness.**
>
> **Yet there is something else**
> **That drags him from his bed;**
> **And he stands in the darkness**

121

With his feet cold against the floor
And the cold air round his ankles.
He does not know why,
But he goes to the window and sees
A beam of light, miles high,
Dividing the night into two before him,
Still, stark and throbbing.

The houses and gardens beneath
Lie under the snow
Quiet and tinged with purple,
There has been no sound of guns,
No roar of exploding bombs;
Only that watchfulness hidden among the snow-covered houses,
And that great beam thrusting back into heaven
The light taken from it.

****

It was during this time that Frank began to realise just how many returned servicemen needed help to adjust to life outside the Army.

Violet herself learned that gender roles were sharply defined in Saskatchewan. Men earned the incomes and handled the finances. Single men had a hard life. Women raised the children, tended the garden, nursed, cooked, and did the hundred and one other tasks needed to provide for home and family. Violet found herself in an environment quite different to what she was used to. (The staple meal of bannocks, beans and bacon was quite new to her).

During this settling-in period a third wave of the Spanish Flu hit Canada, followed by a fourth wave during the winter of 1920 in which women were especially vulnerable. The newspapers continued to report outbreaks of the disease for the next two years. This must have caused considerable worry and concern to every woman with a husband and baby. In addition, this young wife must have been very anxious about her parents so far away. Her father had to regularly meet the public as part of his job. Newly arriving English immigrants in Canada were viewed suspiciously by those who thought that they may be importing the virus.

Whilst acclimatising to her new life, Frank's wife was adapting to living on a reduced income with her sisters-in-law at Larch Avenue. As a married mother in those days, she couldn't go out to work to add to the family income. Whilst unpacking her Singer sewing machine her entrepreneurial qualities came to the fore. She realized that she did have skills that she could capitalize on. She could sew. She could use her adroitness in the house, whilst juggling her share of housekeeping and with looking after baby Betty. She put her ideas to Frank when he came home. In those days many husbands, especially one in Frank's situation, would have felt embarrassed that his wife needed to work. However, he was big enough to gladly accept his wife's offer. The next morning Violet advertised herself as a skilled clothing repairer and seamstress. Before long her every spare moment was, as in had been in England, spent operating her sewing machine.

During September southern Saskatchewan has pleasant weather with average temperatures between 10° to 20° C. However, its climate can be harsh. From December the temperature drops dramatically to reach a freezing, sub-zero average temperature of between -7° and -14° C. It can fall well below -22° C. There are three and a half months of snow each year. In the summertime, temperatures can reach an almost unbearable +40° C. There was no electricity in 1919 and homes were heated during the winter with wood or coal stoves. Lighting was by kerosene lamps.

In this setting the new Hall family eased themselves into Canada's frigid winter. Frank's dark moods continued, and he was often unsympathetic to his wife's concerns. When he was away working, Violet suffered dreadfully from loneliness. She wrote regularly to the family back in England and confessed her unhappiness to her parents. In replying, her father confided, amongst other things, that three of Violet's extended Haslemere family had died unexpectedly during the previous 6 months.

Frank continued to drink too much, and sleep badly. More than once, Violet was disturbed as her husband sobbed in his restlessness. His wartime experiences had affected him more than she had realized. He sometimes cried "Betty, Betty!", and his wife wondered.

Frank realized that Violet was not very enamoured with her new life in Saskatchewan. He perceived a little friction between the women who shared the family home. He thought that it might help if his wife had a home to call her own. Without too much difficulty, he found a house to rent at nearby Redland Avenue. With the help of his brothers, he and Violet moved into the new home in the early springtime of 1920.

During all this upheaval Violet became exhausted as so much had happened during the past few months. Despite her husband being away at work a lot of the time, Violet conceived for her second baby in May of 1920, eight months after her arrival in Moose Jaw. Frank's mother, Annie was living in the town of Superior some 750 miles away in the United States. During the summer of 1920 Violet's new mother-in-law took the long rail journey to visit her family in Moose Jaw. Naturally, she stayed, at the family house in Larch Road. Violet and Annie met often and got along extremely well, becoming close friends. Violet confided that she was finding it hard to adapt to her new life in Canada. Annie, an immigrant herself, quite understood her problems and readily gave Violet sympathy and advice. Violet relied upon Annie's support more than she realized.

During their talks, Violet learned that her new baby would not become a British citizen if born in Canada. The consequence of this news was of great concern to Violet, and she wrote and told her parents. They responded by quickly sending their daughter the money for a return fare back to

England. Frank heard about this turn of events with dismay.

Ten weeks before she was due to give birth, Violet and Betty, in a freezing snowstorm, boarded the train at Moose Jaw station. Few people saw them off. They travelled alone for five days to the trans-Atlantic port of Portland in Maine on the U.S.A. east coast. There on 13th December 1920 they boarded the S.S. Andante, bound for Southampton.

****

Chapter 12

Violet has a Baby Son

My grand-mother's happiness at reaching her parent's home in England was tempered by a natural feeling of being at fault. She felt guilty at leaving her husband alone in Canada, especially over the Christmas period. However, she quickly fitted back into her old routine, making herself indispensable in the home. She helped her mother with the housework, and of course looking after little Betty. Violet's father Charles and her brother 'Boy' worked six days a week at Funnell and Furlongers in Grayshott.

Violet visited the family doctor regularly and the pregnancy progressed well. Old friends and family called around and resumed their affinity. She was made to feel very welcome back in the fold. They introduced their children to Betty and watched as they played happily and got wet and dirty in the stream in the back garden. Soon, apart from a constant nagging of conscience, Violet felt almost as if she had never left Haslemere.

She wrote regularly to Frank, and all seemed to be proceeding as had been expected. During the mid-afternoon on Friday the 18th of February Violet was surprised to see Walter arriving home early. It was so unlike him as he was usually so routine, calm, and unexcitable.

Funnell and Furlonger's vans outside Haslemere station 1920

This time he looked upset and very serious as he addressed his mother and Violet. 'Boy' told them that his father had been taken to hospital, seriously injured. Charles had been kicked by one of his horses whilst examining a hoof. He was 54 years old and had suffered a serious head injury. Violet's baby was due within the next few days.

During the night just seven days later, Violet was sleeping uneasily when she felt pains which she recognised as the onset of her labour. She called out loudly to her brother in the adjoining bedroom. Within two hours the family doctor had arrived and on the morning of Friday 25th of February 1921 her son (my father), was born at home. He was a fit and healthy boy who looked just like his own father Frank. Violet had him baptised a few days later at St Bartholomew's Church. She named him Charles William Frank Sherburn Hall. When he got older, he was usually called Bill. (It was common practice 100 years ago to name children after their family members. In this case it was Charles and William for the baby's grand-fathers, Sherburn after his grandmother and Frank after his father). From the very start, three-years-old Betty took to her tiny brother as if she were his 'mini-mum'.

Whilst this turmoil was going on, Violet still had to tend to her children's needs and be a comfort to her distraught mother Emma. They all constantly worried about Charles in hospital and visited him whenever they could.

Sadly, Charles Furlonger didn't regain consciousness and died with-out leaving hospital three weeks later. This left Violet with very conflicting responsibilities.

By now the family firm's co-owner, Mr Funnell, was too old and infirm to take on the responsibilities of running the business, and Walter stepped up to assume his father's role. He also elected to be his family's breadwinner and provided as well for the Funnell family, as there were no pensions in those days.

('Boy' never married and died at the early age of 64 years. To my mind he displayed a strength of character that set him apart from that which most people are capable. His niece Betty remembered him all her life as a kind, quiet, hardworking, gentleman. That too is how I and my sisters recall him. Very soon after his father died, 'Boy' sold the firms horses and invested in Commer lorries to do the work in their place more safely).

Violet was inundated with interest from former customers but resisted the temptation to take on orders and concentrated on the roles that she already had. Her mother was badly affected by her husband's untimely death. Emma was an intelligent woman but was unhappy and quite lost without Charles and had lapsed into a deep depression.

Soon after 22nd July that year, Violet learned that her maternal grandfather had died unexpectedly in Dorstone. Emma had already lost her own mother. Her depression deepened at the thought of her only grand-children leaving again to live in far off Canada. Violet was in a dilemma. Knowing that she must inevitably leave home, Violet did everything she could think of to help her mother get back onto an even keel before she had to go back to Frank.

On the other side of the Atlantic, Frank's life was evolving separately. His job on the railway involved sorting mail on the trains as they raced across the breadth of Canada. The postal packages often contained valuables, and theft was a considerable temptation to some of the poorly paid clerks. Pilfering losses reflected badly upon the company image, and they had a policy for dealing with it quickly. One day the company learnt that several valuable packages had been stolen. The culprits were unidentified, but the CPR knew that there was a dearth of paid work, and new men could be recruited immediately. The company couldn't afford delay and so Frank's whole crew was summarily sacked. Thus, every man, including Frank, Harry, and Gerald, found themselves without a job.

Before very long ex-Private Harry Hall felt that it was time to follow his dream. Unattached, he took himself eastwards to Toronto on the far-off shores of Lake Ontario. There he was able to secure employment as a staff illustrator for a large newspaper called the Toronto Telegram. His training at art college and the cartoon-drawing skills he had honed during his Army service on the Western Front, were at last to earn him a good living.

Ex-Staff Sergeant Gerald Hall, unlike his brothers, had not suffered from gas poisoning in the war and was relatively fit and healthy. He decided to move in with his married sister Florence, in Conquest. There he found local work on a farm.

Frank remembered the aptitudes he had practiced in his father's business when he was a boy. Eventually after many interviews he found a job as a travelling salesman. He was still based in Moose Jaw and his tools of trade included a model 'T' Ford car which he drove in all weathers to remote places across the prairies. His outgoing personality, engaging manner and fresh good looks made a favourable impression with the lonely homestead housewives, and he was successful at selling.

A Model 'T' Ford car like the one Frank had

After meeting his old friend, businessman Yip Foo from his Militia days, Frank extended his role to include delivering other provisions. Some of his customers lived far from any shops.

He wrote letters to his wife in Haslemere regularly and missed her and little Betty dreadfully. He found it hard to deal alone with his war-time demons, despite a cheerful disposition and his natural inclination to think positively.

Frank however found that his job, travelling extensively, facilitated him visiting ex-soldiers who needed someone to talk to. He felt a strong compelling duty to help them recover from their war experiences. This led to him forming an informal organisation which regularly gave practical help, advice and some solace to men who might otherwise have broken down. Funding was provided by some of the community's wealthy people. This activity went a long way to helping Frank's own state of mind. One of the men that he took under his wing was his old Militia bandsman chum Shaun. He had returned suffering from what a later generation would call Post Traumatic Stress Disorder but was then simply called Shell Shock. Shaun was unable to secure a job and struggled to find the money to feed his family. Frank arranged for some local benefactors to help and advised Shaun how to claim what he could. Mostly though Frank met him regularly and counselled his friend.

Frank was working away from his lodgings for days at a time and found that, through thrift, he could save part of his commissions each week. After twelve months he had managed to save a sizable lump sum.

One evening at home, he looked at his bank statement and realised that he had enough money to put down a deposit on a small house. Most houses in those days were ordered from a catalogue. They were of wooden construction and delivered in kit form. The balance was financed by a mortgage, to be paid off over the proceeding years.

During the early part of 1922, Frank purchased a small plot of land at 474 Hochelaga Street, on the western outskirts of Moose Jaw. He then ordered a modest family house, and it arrived by rail during the early spring. Frank had a local carrier deliver his purchase to the plot that he had bought. Then, as is common in all frontier communities, he and some of his friends working together in their spare time assembled the house. It was completed in just a few weeks. The house proved to be a compact, three-bedroomed home with a small porch. It was then painted and carpeted, before friends and family members donated furniture and fittings. Frank built a wooden fence and started a garden. When the house was ready, Frank wrote and told Violet all about it, describing the house as best as he could without photographs. Three months later, on 1st June 1922, after 16 months away, Violet and her little brood boarded the train taking them to Southampton docks. Thus started the five-day journey back to Moose Jaw.

This time she travelled second class aboard the RMS Andania, which was bound for Montreal.

Chapter 13

"Let's have another go"

As she retraced the long hot rail journey across Canada, Violet had many thoughts on her mind. She was troubled about leaving her mother alone in England and concerned that her brother would find his huge responsibilities too much without her help. She was anxious about the relationship she had with Frank. He had changed so much since they first met at Bramshott. He rarely showed his emotions. She wondered just how much he needed her now, after all that had happened during the past five years.

Although her husband's excessive drinking had never resulted in violence, her protected upbringing had not prepared her for its other behaviours and effects. Secretly she was uncomfortable at the prospect of living on the breadline in the 'back and beyond'. She comforted herself with the knowledge that her two children had both been born in England and so were English subjects and not Canadian. That gave her certain options for the future.

After five interminably scorching days, the train pulled up at Moose Jaw's familiar dusty station. Few other passengers alighted from the carriages onto the platform and this time there was no-one to meet her. She made her way alone to the Hall family home in Larch Avenue. There she surprised her sisters in law Evelyn and Dorothy who had been busy baking in preparation for dinner. The delighted women warmly welcomed Violet back and made a great fuss over baby Bill and naturally of little Betty. Frank however was away working, and not due home from business until the next afternoon.

Sitting in the parlour with Evelyn and Dorothy, Violet was pleased to learn that there was to be a family dinner the next evening. Attending would be Gladys and her husband Wellington, Florence with spouse Fred, accompanied by her brother Gerald and his current girlfriend. Frank of course would have returned from his travels by then, and Harry was arriving on the train from his new home in Toronto. Still unmarried, he often spent his holidays with his Moose Jaw folk. To top it all though was the news that they were to be joined by their parents William and Annie, who were travelling from Superior to stay for two weeks.

Late the next afternoon Violet dressed herself in her nicest cream-coloured summer frock and put on her new and very fashionable yellow sunhat. It was a hot, but lovely day. There was a spring in her step as she pushed the two children in the perambulator the short distance to the Moose Jaw High Street. Carefully selecting a bench in the town's pretty little park, she settled down to gazing at the horizon towards the west. Occasionally checking the time on her broach-watch, she eventually saw that it was five thirty, and nearly time. As the sun slowly sank, Violet squinted and used her hand as a shade from the glare. Firstly, she spotted a black speck which, as she looked, seemed to have a small cloud over it. The speck became a dot and then a square, which after five minutes transposed into a tiny motor car which was bumping over the track towards town. After another few minutes the automobile reached the sealed road at the very start of the High Street. There, this exciting novelty was met by a group of ten or so thrilled children who gave it a tumultuous welcome. The youngsters ran beside the car and two brave smirking boys jumped onto the running boards before it stopped beside an enthusiastically waving Violet.

With a grin that stretched from ear to ear, Frank jumped from the driving seat and rushed over to his wife. His coat covered in dust and still wearing goggles and hat, Frank wrapped his arms around a protesting Violet and kissed her enthusiastically. He then helped her and the children into the car and drove them to the house that he had built in nearby Hochelaga Street. Violet found it a small house in a rough street. Her new home was unfinished on the outside and almost bare of furniture and fittings inside. Violet tried unsuccessfully to hide her disappointment from Frank.

Before they ate that evening Violet sat in the parlour beside Annie and listened to the family's casual unceremonious chattering. Then the happy members all trooped outside to enjoy a camp-fire meal in the garden. Quite different to the Furlongers' polite traditions of dressing for dinner then grace before the other traditional formalities were observed.

After their meal, Violet found herself in the company of her brother-in-law Harry. She had liked Harry from the start and found him easy company. He told her all about his new job as a staff artist in Toronto. As he recounted his tale, Violet felt a stirring of interest in the subject. As a dressmaker, she was an artist of a kind and Harry's enthusiasm for his subject was infectious. This led to Violet being shown the rudiments of observation and some of the secrets of sketching. Their conversations on this topic continued every time Harry came back to Moose Jaw.

Adding homemaking to her jobs of being a mother, wife and dressmaker, Violet settled down to making a success of her marriage. Frank's increased earnings added to her dressmaking renumerations allowed them to make progress in paying off their house mortgage. However, Frank was still away from home too much and this frequently left Violet very alone to look after the children. All too soon the Prairie winter set in again. Violet dreaded the bitter cold which lasted for months. The absolutely essential heating was provided by log fire and the wood had to be delivered or else self-collected from the woods. In those days Saskatchewan houses had no electricity, and from 5 pm to 8 am lighting was provided by oil lamps. It is hard to do intricate needlework or read books by such dim lighting.

Frank thought that he was lucky to have a reasonably well-paid job that he enjoyed and that he was successful at. The country's economy was still in recession, and he knew of many ex-soldiers, returned from the war, who had to work at the very best as unskilled labourers. There was little official help for men who had come home with wounds. Life especially with severe physical and/or mental injuries was usually faced with the stoicism typical of the times. However, fortitude didn't feed your family.

In his work Frank met a lot of wealthy townspeople and farmers who had not left Canada for various, usually justified, reasons. They all knew and often thought well of Herbert Snell and of Frank's father who had worked for the Colonel. These people were very interested in Frank's experiences overseas. Frank used this opportunity to elicit their help in building up his locally funded support group for ex-servicemen who needed help. Frank's involvement in this charitable work took up a lot of his time and energy. He also kept in touch with the ex-Bramshott nurses who had similar interests in nearby Regina. All of this involvement did nothing to ease the growing friction between Violet and Frank.

Every few months Frank's mother visited Moose Jaw from Superior for a week or so and Violet looked forward to seeing her very much. For the rest of the time, she was dependent for female company upon seeing Evelyn, Dorothy, and Gladys. Edith living 100 miles away, rarely came to Moose Jaw.

Frigid winters alternated with hot summers. It was problematic for Violet to leave the house with the children during the winter months due to the snow. Being a new development, the street where they lived was unmade and during the melt it turned to mud. She mended clothes for the neighbouring loggers and First Nation families. Occasionally Violet was commissioned to make dresses for the more prosperous people in town. She found that she had little in common with either neighbours or customers. Sometimes she felt that they didn't like her English accent.

My grandmother brooded in her loneliness and wondered if it was really necessary for Frank to be absent so much.

The war had finished years previously and she could not understand why he visited and drank with men from his Army days so frequently. She also knew that Frank was an attractive man and that he was popular. She was only too aware that some of his customers and contacts lived isolated lives miles away from town.

At the age of five, Betty was enrolled into her nearby school for the start of the 1924 term. Being an outgoing child, she soon settled into the routine and made many friends. Betty was walked to school by her mum each day. Violet missed her company without her. She increased her efforts to become more acquainted with the neighbours.

In the spring of that year Frank's brother Harry made one of his regular visits to see the family in Moose Jaw. Bill was only three, but bonny Betty was five. She had masses of blond curly hair and an inquisitive confident nature.

Harry was straight-away entranced and spent a lot of time with his delightful little niece. He soon introduced Betty to his style of cartoon drawing and was thrilled when she showed an immediate talent.

Violet outside her Moose Jaw house with Bill ("Buster") 1923

Violet with Betty and "Buster" outside their home in 1923

(As she grew up Betty continued with this interest and as a teenager went to art school. She qualified and practiced as an art teacher at a prestigious school until she married).

Soon, because she wanted to be like her schoolmates, Betty persuaded her parents to buy her a pony. From then on, she rode the two miles to and from her lessons with her friends.

Betty Hall (aged six)

Bill wasn't neglected by his father either. One fine, sunny but cold winter's day his dad hitched a big wooden sledge to the back of the Ford car. He then lifted Bill and some of his warmly dressed friends up into the car. While Violet watched anxiously from the house, Frank drove off to the Moose Jaw River. Parking up on firm ground, he led the boys towards some large logging vehicles with which the men were working. The little boys squatted down and watched fascinated as the frozen river water was cut into huge blocks of ice. After a while the burly foreman called to Frank and invited him to bring the boys down to the bank. Once there they were shown a pile of waste ice chunks of various sizes. Inside each was a frozen fish, and the excited little boys were allowed to choose one piece each to take home. *(Every aspect of this day out was recounted to me fifty years later)*.

On a summer's morning in 1925, whilst Frank was away for several days on a work trip, four-year-old Bill went out to play with his street chums. When he didn't come home for lunch Violet was unconcerned as it was often the case that he would have his meal at the house of one of his little chums. She became a little anxious when he didn't come home in time for tea. Becoming more concerned as the evening progressed, Violet called on her neighbours asking after Bill. She carried on making increasingly frantic enquiries until it got dark. No-one had seen her little boy. Frank was not due home until the next evening and Violet had Betty to care for. She didn't know what to do. She had no telephone and she sat up all night, worried sick.

The next morning in desperation, she went with Betty to school, and asked the teacher, what course of action she could take. It was not the first time that the teacher had been asked this sort of question. Her immediate response was, "Go and report it at the RCMP post in town straight away!"

Hailing down a passing cab Violet, feeling by now quite sick with worry, was within half an hour at the downtown Police Station. A full detailed report later, Violet hurried off to the Hall family home in Larch Avenue to tell Evelyn and Dorothy of her distress.

The Police straight away organised searches of the riverbank and other places where children played. Enquiries were made at all of the neighbouring houses, and at the end of that first day Violet was visited by an experienced detective. She was advised to post a reward locally for the safe return of little Billy. Violet arranged for that to be done and went home as instructed to wait for news. At this time, she felt very alone and missed her husband's support very keenly. She sobbed by herself until she fell into a troubled sleep.

The next morning, the exhausted Violet was getting Betty ready for school when she heard a knock on her front door. She rushed to answer it and found a uniformed officer with his police car outside the house. With heart in mouth she listened, and her knees felt weak when she was told that Bill had just been brought into the Police station. So without delay, Violet and Betty were ushered into the car. First Betty was dropped off at school and then her mother was driven straight to the station. The reunion between mother and son can be imagined. Only then was Violet introduced to a young woman who stood shyly in the office. It was explained to Violet that the native girl had brought Billy to the station early that morning, having found him "wandering around lost". She now expected her promised reward. Violet reached quickly to open her handbag, but her hand was stayed by the officer who said, *"No, Mrs. Hall, not money, she will spend it on grog. Take her to the store and buy her some supplies. That will be better".*

So that is the course of action that Violet took. Although she was generous in her purchases, the girl was most displeased not to receive the expected cash. Only after she left did Violet see that Bill was wearing an old pair of moccasins and that his new leather boots were missing. *(Another*

134

story recounted to me in the 1970s)

Whilst this drama was unfolding, Frank was driving across the prairies on his way home to Moose Jaw. With a grin on his face, he lustily sang to himself an old familiar song:

"It's a long way to Tipperary, it's a long way to go.
It's a long way to Tipperary, to the sweetest girl I know.
Good-bye Piccadilly,
Farewell Leicester Square.
It's a long, long way to Tipperary, but my heart's right there".

He was happily looking forward to sharing good news with Violet.

(When Frank had picked up his pay packet, it had contained a letter from head office. His eyes had widened as he read that he was being offered a promotion. He was to be the area manager and get a sizable pay increase. That would perhaps enable him and Violet to afford a better house nearer to the centre of the town. Almost as good was that, with the help of his business friends and the Regina nurses, he had at last found a decent job for his old mate Shaun. He was to be taken on as a porter at the Regina hospital).

Frank couldn't wait to tell his wife. "That will make her happy!" he thought to himself. As he approached Moose Jaw he was unaware of the frightful time that Violet had been through. He was a little surprised when he passed the town park to see that Violet wasn't waiting for him as was her custom. When he reached home, he was greeted by his son Bill who was hiding in his little den underneath the house to escape the summer heat. Bill was playing cowboys with his toy gun. Frank gave him a cuddle and then strode into the house to see that Violet was sitting at the kitchen table clutching a handkerchief, with tears in her eyes. Frank assumed that she had been missing him, and that she needed cheering up. He knew just what to tell her.

When Frank had finished blurting out his happy story, he was puzzled by his wife's reaction. She was not pleased at what he had said at all. She burst into tears again, and through them told Frank what had taken place at home while he had been away. Nonplussed, Frank replied that of course he was pleased that Billy was back and unharmed, but his puzzled response wasn't what was needed. What Violet longed for, was an empathy that her husband was quite unable to understand or emotionally, to provide. Instead, Frank, very tired after is long drive, sighed and poured himself his first glass of rye.

All too soon, and before Frank and Violet had enough saved up to change their home, the cold winter weather began again. While the wind howled, Violet was in regular correspondence with family and friends in Haslemere. It filled the long hours.

Her mother was not coping well without her Charles, and she still seemed very desolate. This worried Violet and she also felt that she should be there to help her only sibling 'Boy'. He also wrote and described being inundated with work issues. Violet, stuck in the Canadian prairies, increasingly felt a keen sense of divided loyalties.

Towards the end of January 1926, Annie Elizabeth came to visit her family in frigid Saskatchewan from Superior city. She and Violet were delighted to see each other again. Violet confided her troubles to her mother-in-law, who promised help and support.

Before she caught the train to see her daughter Edith in Conquest, the older woman assured Violet that she would speak to her son who was working in the area.

Three weeks later, whilst on that visit, Annie Elizabeth, aged just 67, suddenly died. She was the matriarch whose quite unexpected death was felt very keenly by her whole extended family. Annie's body was brought back to Moose Jaw by train, and she was buried in the town cemetery on 30th February 1926. Hundreds of townsfolk attended.

Violet, Bill, Betty, and two young friends in Moose Jaw 1925

To lose her anchor and friend so abruptly, was the very final straw for Violet. She had to visit her mum.

****

Chapter 14

The End and the Beginning.....!

Early one sunny morning at the end of May 1926 Frank took his young family to the rail station in the Ford. After helping them and their travel bags onto their carriage he kissed his nearest and dearest goodbye.

__Frank's daughter Betty was 7½, and Billy only 5__

The next three months was going to be a lonely time for their dad. Violet was very quiet, and Frank put it down to the sadness of their separation. He planned to make progress with the new house while his family were away.

As Violet's rail carriage was drawn the long, long miles towards Canada's east coast, she suffered from very mixed emotions. She was excited at the thought of presenting her beautiful children to her mother Emma. She was keen to see England again and renew her friendships there. In addition, she was anxious as to whether the family business was too much for her brother to cope with on his own. 'Boy' was now over 30 years old and had not been afforded the social time to find himself a wife.

Five days after leaving Moose Jaw, the train arrived at Montreal Station. After gaining the thronging platform, the tired but excited children and their mother were transported to the docks. Soon they were climbing the long gangway up onto the huge, towering deck of the SS Minnedosa. There they were greeted by a porter and shown to their cabin. Before breakfast the next morning, the great ship quietly slipped her moorings and headed directly eastwards, accelerating towards the rising sun.

The weather during the five days spent crossing the Atlantic Ocean was warm, and the seas calm. Violet spent most of her time trying to relax on deck watching her little ones capering, frolicking, and romping about with the other children. She arranged with the ship's communications office for a telegram to be sent to her brother, advising him when the ship was due to dock at Southampton. Violet tossed and turned in her bed each night but found that sleep largely evaded her.

On the morning of Thursday, 10th June 1926, Violet got washed and dressed long before the children were awake. She had a lot of packing to do. Much later, after they had all breakfasted, the Minnedosa tied up at the, familiar to Violet, Southampton docks. Once all the formalities were over, the three of them were met in the reception hall by Violet's smiling brother Boy, who had come to take them home.

'Boy' and his dog Curley

During the two-hour drive in Funnell and Furlonger's little lorry, Betty and Billy had their noses pressed to the glass as they watched the lovely countryside unfold before their eyes. So very different from Saskatchewan's bare flatness. As 'Boy' negotiated the winding roads with practiced ease, Violet felt more relaxed as they caught up with news.

Bill in 'Boy's' van

The brakes squealed contentedly as their transport stopped softly on the road outside "Weybrook". A smiling Emma was standing just beside the front door to welcome her only daughter back home again.

During the next fortnight, Violet was so busy and involved that she barely had time to think. Weybrook was in a mess, and she was puzzled as her mother was usually fastidious about housework. Violet spent a whole day putting the house right. The next day she visited the local school and arranged for the children to start there on the following Monday. Soon neighbours and family heard that she was home and began a social round of visits.

After a week had gone by, Violet realised that she had been so preoccupied that she had neglected to write to Frank. When she began to do so she found some difficulty in composing the words and completing the letter. But she filled it in by writing at length about how the children were settling into their new Surrey schools. He soon replied but their letters back and forth were stilted and constrained. They had lost the easy flow of literary affection that they once had.

After she had the house and children sorted out, Violet talked at length

139

with her brother about the state of the family business. Book-keeping had never been one of his strengths, and so Violet took that task upon herself.

Soon old dressmaking customers were calling at Weybrook to place orders. Within a few weeks Violet bought herself a new Singer and began to take on work. One day she answered the front door to find Mabel Dolmetsche smiling at her. The two women had missed each other and talked long over their tea. Eventually Violet was persuaded to resume making clothing for her friend. During their chats Mabel enthused about her forthcoming ancient dance and musical performances. Violet felt a pang as she realised how she had missed the culture she had been used to. When she was offered gratis tickets to the exhibitions, she was quick to request additional tickets for her very bright daughter to attend as well.

Betty's schoolteachers were the same ladies who had taught Violet as a child. They teased their newest pupil by telling her that she wasn't as smart at school as her mother had been. Betty's schoolmates tormented her about her strong Canadian accent. However, this tough girl reacted to all of this by working harder and consequently she excelled at her lessons. Betty found that walking the two miles to school and back in all weathers was easy, although she did miss her little Canadian pony.

Frank's daughter went whenever she had the chance, to the Dolmetsch's concerts. If there was any other kind of musical concert performed at the Haslemere town hall, Violet somehow found the money needed for tickets. Mabel liked Betty and before long she gifted Betty a valuable Dolmetsche violin. A love of classical music was born in Betty, which lasted all of her life.

Six months after arriving back in Haslemere, Violet realized that she didn't want to leave. She shuddered at the thought of the flat featureless prairie, the pioneer lifestyle, the approaching Saskatchewan winter, and Frank's emotional distance. She felt that he just wasn't the same man that she had fallen in love with at Bramshott Camp nine years before. "Maybe he would be different if he joined me in England?" she thought. The next day Violet wrote to her husband and explained that she wasn't going to leave Haslemere. She urged Frank to come over and make his future in the Furlonger's family business. He had after all been born in England and had siblings who lived in the country. She wanted her husband to join her and make a new life for himself away from the job that took him away from his family so much.

Three weeks later Violet had her reply. Frank wrote that he felt that he had done everything that he was reasonably capable of to provide for her and the children. Further he thought that she was betraying him by staying in England and he believed that by taking the children from him, Violet had left by deceit. He believed that she had not tried hard enough to embrace the new life that she had married into. Inside he felt heartbroken but was quite unable to put into words his very wretched and hurt feelings. He expressed no sympathy or understanding for her emotions in the matter. They never wrote to each other again.

My grandmother's belief that Frank was a cold uncaring man, was reinforced in her mind by his words in this last letter.

During that winter Frank's sisters Evelyn and Dorothy visited England from Moose Jaw. It was said to be a very rare holiday to visit their English siblings. Because their ship docked at Southampton, they included a visit to their sister-in-law and her children and hoped to persuade Violet to return to Frank in Canada.

Evelyn and Dorothy stayed at an hotel in Haslemere near to where Violet lived. Whatever was said between these women when they met, entrenched the position between the two families and ended in acrimony. It was the last contact that Violet had with her Canadian family.

She determined to devote her attention to her responsibilities in Haslemere. In this she did a superb job for the rest of her life, as a business-woman, as a mother, and in later life as a carer to her mother Emma and as a grandmother.

Violet's children were bright and did well at all their school subjects. Betty felt compelled to follow her dream and become an artist, in the footsteps of her uncle Harry. In 1934, when she was sixteen, she enrolled at an art college in Guildford to continue her studies.

When Bill was fifteen, he took the highly competitive examination to enter the Halton Royal Air Force Apprentices School near Aylesbury in Buckinghamshire. This tested his knowledge, intelligence, aptitude, and medical condition. He passed and sought to qualify in radio telegraphy like his father Frank had been before him.

Betty's sketch of Roger and his children drawn in 1980

In 1936, after a two-year qualifying course, Betty began a ten-year career as an art teacher in English private schools. Throughout World War

Two she taught at a prestigious boarding school near Totness in Devon called Dartington Hall. It was an extremely progressive school and very controversial. In her choice she may well have been influenced by her contact with the very bourgeois Dolmetsch family.

Her brother Bill successfully completed his three-year apprenticeship in 1939, just in time to play his part in the Second World War. At the age of eighteen he had qualified in a cutting-edge technology and was now a radar engineer. His first posting was to RAF St Morgan in Cornwall where he assisted in maintaining Coastal Command aircraft.

These aeroplanes flew day and night convoy protection sorties, dangerously deep across the Atlantic.

During 1940, Betty became friendly with 18-year-old Eunice Rachel Cohen (Pat), who worked as a children's nurse at Dartington Hall school. Betty introduced Pat to her brother Bill at a dance, and the two got along very well with each other straight away. They met up whenever their work and duties allowed, and Pat became smitten by this handsome confident young Airman. Bill was at that time anticipating a posting to the Far East and hated the thought of leaving this very pretty girl behind. One evening on the spur of the moment, after some drinks, he asked Pat to marry him. They hardly knew each other, but it was wartime and, like his parents before him they couldn't guarantee the future. Pat was terrified that if the Germans did invade England, as most people feared was imminent, she with her very Jewish name would be targeted by them. She was terrified that she would be sent to a camp. She didn't know of any other way to get an English name. On the 6th of May 1941, when Bill was just 20 and Pat still only 18 years old, this very unworldly and naive couple married at the little St. Austell parish church. Their first child, Terry Anne, was born the next year. When Bill was posted to Dambulla in Ceylon as part of 217 Squadron RAF a few months later, his wife's headmaster allowed Pat to stay working at Dartington Hall and look after her baby for the remainder of the war. My mother was often seen in her leisure time cycling about the countryside with laughing baby Terry in the front basket.

During 1944, Betty and Bill's grandmother Emma was found to be suffering from dementia. Violet redoubled her own efforts to include being her mother's carer, but Emma died two years after her illness had been diagnosed.

In early 1946, with the war over, twenty-five-year-old Bill (now known by his friends as Nobby) returned to England. After over three years of continuous service overseas, he was now a hugely experienced Warrant Officer. He had changed considerably from the 20-year-old who had married his 18-year-old bride.

Pat had also grown up, bearing the responsibilities and making all the family decisions. She had now been a working single mother for four years. (As they both later in life told me "After all that time, we barely knew each other").

There was a massive shortage of housing for returning servicemen. However, Bill was a lateral thinker and soon bought an old bus which he converted into a comfortable mobile home and parked up in a field on the perimeter of his RAF camp.

The only water available was that taken from the nearby drainage ditch and then boiled before being used. Just nine months after Bill's return, their second child (Roger) was born. He came into the world suffering from an infection caused by the impure water used to make up his milk formula. This caused a lack of oxygen reaching his brain resulting in his skin having a blue tinge. (Blue baby syndrome or methemoglobinemia).

Pat's third child arrived ten months after Roger was born. Bill and his wife lived in their 'bus' for the first two years after their reunification.

Mark and Jo Walton now live in Australia

Betty meanwhile tired of the post-war British austerity, and in 1946 emigrated to far off New Zealand. Once settled in Christchurch, she married a lovely man called John Walton. They had three sons. Her first was called Bill after her brother. Sadly, he died when he was quite young.

Tony Walton, still lives with Hazel in New Zealand

As the other two boys grew up, Betty introduced them to her love of classical music. It was in their blood and they both excelled beyond all expectations in their musical careers.

Pat's eldest daughter Terry became a well-regarded school head teacher. Roger joined the Royal Armoured Corps and became a communications specialist like his father and grandfather before him.

Terry, Roger and Sue

He went on to spend 32 years as a policeman, firstly in the New Zealand Police and later in England. Sue had a long and rewarding career in accounts with Citroen UK.

Nanna, Terry, and Roger 1948

Some years after Violet left him, Frank remarried and had a successful and happy life. He and his new wife had two daughters and so initiated a whole new (Canadian) branch of the Sherburn Hall family. Frank died in Montreal, Quebec when he was 84 years old.

'Boy' died when he was 64 years old in 1960. He never married and left everything he had to his sister.

As children, I, my sisters, and my New Zealand cousins had a close and loving relationship with our Nanna.

__Me visiting Nanna at Weybrook during the summer of 1951__

__Violet Hall on her way to see Betty in New Zealand in 1961__

Violet died on the 4th of April 1977, when she was 83 years old.

Now with my own 75 years of life experiences and having completely unravelled Violet's ball of khaki wool, I appreciate her full story. I understand what factors caused her to part with Frank. A man she had loved so much, but who had been changed irrevocably by his experiences in war.

She is now with her brother 'Boy', and with her parents Emma and Charles. They are buried together at Saint Bartholomew's Churchyard, Derby Road, Haslemere.

ALSO OF THEIR S T
CHAPLES WALTER
APRIL 13 1960
ACED 4 YEARS
ALSO THEIR DAUGHTER
VIOL T HALL
AGED 83 YE RS

* * * * * * * * * * * * * * * * * * *

Postscript

JASPER'S NOSE

"Happy birthday", he whispered. My granddaughter kneeled encouragingly behind her little son in case he lost his nerve. My gnarled, hard worked hands clumsily accepted the neat package from his little pink fingers. I turned my head slowly to take in the sea of smiling, sympathetic, familiar faces that surrounded me in the private ward. As the shy-boy scampered away in relief, I struggled slowly with, "Why, thank-you, err, young fella". My memory isn't as good as it once was, but long-ago things are crystal clear.

Jasper

I used to scamper everywhere when I was a boy. Jasper was my dog. He had big floppy ears and a tongue that wet your whole face if you didn't watch out. At night I often lay listening to the great wind as it howled over the wide frozen river and shrieked off into the silent blackness of the snow-burdened forests. Beneath my bed, Jasper's mysterious doggy dreams, with its whimpers, woofs and whines, comforted me.

I dreaded the morning. I had to start school. Mama said so.

The very name "Moose Jaw" frightened me. After our breakfast my big sister Betty nagged, "now come along Silly Billy, put your boots on, it's time we set out". I dragged out every chore, while Jasper rubbed his nose against my leg in sympathy. But Mama knew us only too well, and I was ushered out, squinting in the bright blue sunlight. Freshly fallen snow half-hid the log-pile and muffled the clip-clop of Betty's horse's hooves. I smelt the cold, the wood smoke, and the raw emptiness of the land. I heard my dog scratching to be let out to be with me. For a while I kicked the snow into little piles with my new boots, then up, up, up so high, I was hoisted onto the big horse's rump. Betty settled her ample behind importantly into the saddle, then half-turned and told me, "Now hold onto my belt Billy, and do stop that snivelling". We set off on my reluctant journey to 'The Jaw'.

My Mama had taken me to the school once before. I had to leave Jasper behind. The teacher was tall and crabby. She didn't smile. She wasn't kind. She and Mama talked about me as if I wasn't there. They looked at me now and then as they talked. I stood there twisting my fingers while the boys and girls looked at me. One girl with red hair put her tongue out, and I looked down. I didn't like it there and wished I was at home with Jasper.

As we reached the hump of the hill, by the broken cart, I turned and looked back. Smoke drifted lazily from the chimney and Mama was already feeding the breakfast leftovers to the hens. A terrible loneliness overcame me, and my insides hurt so much that I cried, and cried, and cried. Betty said nothing. I cried for a long time. Then I sobbed. Then I was quiet. Then I got mad.

"No!", I thought suddenly, "I won't go to school. I am going to run away!" We were trotting along a rutted track through trees, and my big sister had taken to singing softly to take her mind off my complaining. Ahead I saw where a drift covered the trail. When we reached it, Betty clicked her tongue and moved her ankles and reins to guide the horse past the obstacle. As the horse slowed down to step carefully through the deep drift, I quickly slid off his rump, hoping that the big metal shoes wouldn't kick me. As I fell, I lost my new slate and my woolly hat, and I lay quietly on my back for a few moments completely covered by whiteness. After a while I straightened up. Betty was quite a way off and she hadn't noticed me missing. This was like a game of hide and seek and I quickly scurried off to hide behind a nearby tree. I half expected to hear her stern voice ordering me back. When I next peeked, Betty and the horse were gone, and I was alone.

"Not going to that old school!", I said over and over again, jumping and dancing with the joy of a newly escaped prisoner. Then I began to walk back the way we had come, towards home. I knew what I was doing was naughty, but maybe when she saw me, my Mama would love me, like she did when I was little. The sky was grey now and I saw the first big flake fall lazily and silently, to join the heavy blanket, already covering the ground.

As I walked my new boots squeaked, and soon my toes felt sore. The first flake turned to lots, and then there were so many falling that I couldn't see very far. It was difficult to spot where the horse's passage had disturbed the snow. It was being covered over like sprinkled sugar hides the cracks in freshly cooked cake. I didn't notice the wind's arrival at first. I did though when my head prickled with the cold, and I missed my new woolly hat. I heard the familiar swish and sway of trees being bent. I felt the first pangs of fear.

After a long time, I reached the top of a hill and squinted to look down at my home. Just discernible was the log wall, half covered by a deep drift. I was so happy knowing that my Mama would be waiting for me in the kitchen. I could curl up in her arms and she would tell me that I was a "Silly Billy" and hug me close. I was so cold, that I ran clumsily and urgently down the hill towards warmth.

"Someone has moved the broken cart!", I thought, as I slipped and slithered through the whiteness. When I reached the riverside, there was only a pile of logs. A pile like the loggers leave all over the place. I stood and looked around me in confusion. Where was home? Where was Mama? I was so cold. I was a little boy lost.

Even children have an instinct for survival and before long I had wedged and snuggled myself into a space between the logs in the pile. There out of the wind and sheltered from the icy wind, I curled up and sucked my fingers and cried. At last, I fell asleep.

Being a country boy, I knew about the animals that lived in the forests. I had even seen a few wolves at a distance. Once my dog had got very excited at the smells around a fir tree. He wouldn't come when I called him, so I went to get him. When I got close-up, I saw great claw marks had ripped the tree trunk, and I felt small and frightened. Never more scared in my whole life, I ran all the way home. Breathlessly I told Mama about what I had seen, in a gushing panting rush. She warned me never to go so far into the forest again.

I started suddenly, instantly alert. My hands hurt with the cold, but that wasn't why I had woken up. The shiver I felt was accompanied by the sheer primitive terror of the prey. I held my breath. There was a noise outside, and it wasn't the wind. It was a grunt. Trying to make myself as small as possible, I squeezed even further into the tiny space. The grunting changed into the hoarse urgent panting of a large animal. I cried out in desperate fright. A shadow passed in front of me, and I heard the rasping squeak of fresh snow being pushed aside by something dark and strong and determined. Soon, hot putrid breath hit my face and I screamed a final "Mama!"

Jasper's warm wet nose hit my face and my arms instinctively wrapped around his woolly neck. His huge tongue competed with his

151

floppy ears, to greet me. I laughed and cried with relief, both at the same time. Big gentle hands lifted me out and wrapped me up in warm blankets, that smelled of home. I was carried the 100 yards from the log pile to the kitchen, whilst Jasper pranced and woofed with happiness. Mama only said with kindness edging her quiet voice, "Where have you been? We have been worried about you Silly Billy"?

Now after a lifetime, I looked across the room at 'The Shy Boy', and I determined to buy him a Jasper for his next birthday. Some folks need a dog more than others and I owe my dog everything.

(Written by me in 1997 for my father, shortly before he died).

Note 1: Half a Crown

Late during the late misty evening of Saturday 12th December 1936, Bert was driving his lorry back to the Funnell and Furlonger yard in Grayshott, after a delivery in Guildford. He changed down to a lower gear as he negotiated the winding hill up the Devil's Punchbowl to the Hindhead crossroad. There was little traffic. He noted that his headlights became less bright as his speed decreased, but he knew that the big alternator provided sufficient lighting for safety.

Glancing casually into his rear-view mirror Bert saw a car's dim headlights right behind him. Cars often used to take advantage of bigger vehicles better lights in those days, as their smaller engines produced much reduced lighting at low speeds. Bert juggled his gears and accelerator to allow the following car to stay close.

Reaching the crossroad at the top of the hill, Bert pulled over to allow his engine to cool down. As he rolled himself a cigarette, he noticed that the big car had also pulled over. His eyes widened when he saw that it was a very opulent black limousine.

A Daimler E20 limousine from 1936

As he looked, he saw that a livered chauffeur got out from behind the driving wheel and walked towards him. In the dim light, Bert caught the emerging sight of polished knee length boots, jodhpurs, smart cap, and buttoned black jacket. Then the apparition reached his lorry's door. Winding down his window, Bert stuttered, "Can I help?" The chauffeur grinned and handed Bert a coin, saying "My master thanks you for helping us up the hill." Bert looked and saw that it was a half crown that he had been given. Before he could say anything, the man had returned to the sleek limousine, which then left in the direction of Portsmouth.

In those days people followed the news by reading the newspapers. When Bert got home, he re-read his Saturday morning paper headlines. The penny dropped! This humble driver only then realized that he had helped the abdicated King Edward VIII on his way to exile in France.

****

About the Author

Roger Sherburn-Hall

In early 1946 my father Bill returned from the Far East after serving almost four years there in Royal Air Force. I was born 10 months after he and my mother were re-united. As such I came into the world at the start of the UK's post war population boom. I therefore truly qualify as a "Boomer".

Baby Boomers are said to have eight common characteristics:

- A strong work ethic.
- Self-assurance.
- Goal centricity.
- Resourcefulness.
- Mental focus.
- Team orientated.
- Disciplined.

So, I wonder, where did I go wrong?????

As a "Service Brat" I went to about seven schools and was often the tubby new boy. However, looking back, I recall those days mostly with pleasure. It taught me how to cope when others "stuck their tongue out at me". I find that attribute to be very useful to this day!

At 15, I craved a motorbike but had little money, only a paper round earnings. My parents who had previously each had their own set of wheels, were naturally fearful and said that I would have to pay out of my own pocket for my dream. (Thinking I would be put off!). My plan was to start a window cleaning round. Mum and Dad promised to pay half of the money for a ladder but told me that I would have to pay the money back. My window cleaning round was quite profitable and achieved my aim. As a result, watched anxiously by my mother, I rode my 250cc BSA (badly) for a year. Predictably I eventually crashed the bike but emerged (typically), relatively unscathed!

When I left school at 16, my dad wanted me to be an engineer, whilst my mum said she'd arranged for me to attend a quantity surveyor interview. Boring! ... I wanted to be a journalist with the Andover Advertiser. My classmate Barry Wheeler (later to become the Editor-in-Chief of Australian Associated Press) got the job as cub-reporter and I joined Burtons Menswear as a junior salesman! Most of my wages were commission and so I learned (very quickly) how to be a confident talker.

Reaching 17, I was on my way to work when I did a double take as I passed the Army Recruiting Office window. Less than a year later, I was serving in Aden as a very junior Trooper in an armoured car regiment! Following that year, I enjoyed 7 years as a member of the British Army on the Rhine. Being now a married man, I left and joined the New Zealand Police. In the Antipodes, I had a fascinating five years, serving in Wellington, Timaru, Auckland and Great Barrier Island, before returning to England via three months in Australia. Back in England I pulled on a different uniform and toiled for the next 28 years as a member the Hampshire Police. Along the way I had three sons but after a 30-year marriage I became divorced, and then my eldest son Alan sadly died in 2008. Thirty months after that I remarried.

My police career ended 16 years ago when quite unexpectedly I had a heart attack. Since then, I have been taking it easy at often part-time work. I started up a small business, combined with working for the Probation Service, crewing an ambulance, being a civilian employee for the Police, driving a minibus, and operating as a taxi driver. Now that I am retired, I exercise other people's dogs, walk long distances, and visit the local Leisure Centre to keep fit. I drive people to medical appointments and deliver the Parish magazine. When I have nothing to do, my wife Ann helpfully finds something for me to be occupied with.

I have become increasingly interested in my Grandmother Violet's life and times as my life progressed. Like most people, I wish I had persisted in asking my forebears about their first-hand memories. I have always liked writing, and now I have written my first book. I am enjoying every minute of the journey.

Roger Sherburn-Hall

Printed in Great Britain
by Amazon

77998439R00093